PUFFIN BOOKS

SURVIVE IN TIME

DAVE REAR

SURVIVE IN TIME

THE SEVEN WONDERS OF THE ANCIENT WORLD

Illustrated by ADAM MING

PUFFIN

PUFFIN BOOKS

UK | USA | Canada | Ireland | Australia
India | New Zealand | South Africa

Puffin Books is part of the Penguin Random House group of companies
whose addresses can be found at global.penguinrandomhouse.com

www.penguin.co.uk   www.puffin.co.uk   www.ladybird.co.uk

Penguin
Random House
UK

First published in Great Britain by Puffin Books 2025

001

Printed and bound in Great Britain by Clays Ltd

The authorized representative in the EEA is Penguin Random House Ireland,
Morrison Chambers, 32 Nassau Street, Dublin D02 YH68

A CIP catalogue record for this book is available from the British Library

ISBN: 978-0-241-74067-5

All correspondence to:
Puffin Books, Penguin Random House Children's
One Embassy Gardens, 8 Viaduct Gardens, London SW11 7BW

MIX
Paper | Supporting
responsible forestry
FSC® C018179

Penguin Random House is committed to a
sustainable future for our business, our readers
and our planet. This book is made from Forest
Stewardship Council® certified paper.

For Ma and Pa

CONTENTS

Ever wondered what it would be like to explore the Great Pyramid of Giza and almost get eaten by a mummy? Or to sneak into the Hanging Gardens of Babylon while being chased by a bunch of angry guards? How about to visit the Mausoleum of Halicarnassus and think, like all visitors to the Mausoleum of Halicarnassus, *what on* earth *is a mausoleum?*

If the answer to any of these questions is *yes*, or just *maybe*, or even *not really but now you come to mention it*, then this is the book for you! Thanks to the time machine provided by Intrepid Explorers Inc., you can visit all Seven Wonders of the Ancient World. But this is no ordinary time-travelling adventure. This is one where YOU get to make the decisions and choose where to go, what to do and how to survive in time.

STRAP YOURSELF IN. YOUR SAFE RETURN IS ABSOLUTELY NOT GUARANTEED.

THE STORY OF THE SEVEN WONDERS OF THE ANCIENT WORLD

Lots of people have heard of the Seven Wonders of the Ancient World. But if you asked them to name all seven, I bet you they couldn't. Why don't you try it with your mum or dad now? My guess is they'll come up with one or two, maybe three or four if they're a bit geeky.

These are the ones they *should* know: the Great Pyramid of Giza and the Hanging Gardens of Babylon.

These are the ones they *might* know: the Colossus of Rhodes and the Lighthouse of Alexandria.

And these last three are the ones they will probably only know if they've studied the ancient wonders or if they're so incredibly old they were actually alive thousands of years ago when the wonders were built: the Statue of Zeus at Olympia, the Temple of Artemis at Ephesus and the Mausoleum of Halicarnassus. I mean, the *what at where?*

How would YOU like to explore each one?

Since, of all the Seven Wonders, only the Great Pyramid of Giza survives today, we're going to need a time machine for this journey. Luckily for you, I have one. And I'm willing to let you ride in it for, say, the price of this book. (But if you borrowed this book from a library, don't worry, you can still come. Libraries are great.)

As the chief pilot of Intrepid Explorers Inc., I'll be your guide on this time-travelling adventure. But before we begin our mission, let's learn where the idea of the Seven Wonders came from. Who thought up the list? Why did they choose these places in particular? And why did they not decide on somewhere more fun, like Disneyland or Pizza Hut?

We're not sure who the very first person to make a list of the world's Seven Wonders was, but the most famous was created by Antipater of Sidon, who lived around 100 BCE. He came up with the list as a kind of guide for travellers. He actually called the places on the list 'sights', but the Greek word for 'sights' (*theamata*) was similar to the one for 'wonders' (*thaumata*), so people must have got confused.

Later, other Greek writers including Strabo and Diodorus also mentioned the Seven Wonders in their works. They always said there were seven – not six, or eight or ten. Seven has always been considered a special number. There are seven days in the week, seven colours in the rainbow, seven seas on Earth and, of course, seven dwarves. We clearly like the number seven.

That doesn't mean there weren't *more* than seven wonders in ancient times. But the Greeks only knew about the civilizations in their part of the world. If they had travelled all over the globe, they might have chosen other places like Petra, an amazing underground city in Jordan in the Middle East, or the Great Wall of China, which eventually extended to an incredible 13,000 miles long! But they didn't know about them yet. (And if Pizza Hut had been around 3,000 years ago, I'm sure it would've been on the list too.)

Before we explore each of the official Seven Wonders of the Ancient World, I'll tell you what you need to know about each one – it's not a good idea to land a time machine in a place you know nothing about. That's how accidents happen. You won't know my friend Joshua, who borrowed one of our time machines without permission and went to ancient Greece. And the reason you won't know Joshua is because . . . he's still in ancient Greece. You get the picture.

But after we land at our destination, you'll be on your own. You'll have to make decisions yourself about which direction to go and what to do. Be careful! Make the wrong choice and you might end up locked in a dungeon, thrown off a mountain or eaten by massive rats. Life was dangerous in the ancient world.

But I'm sure you'll be fine . . .

BUCKLE UP.
LET'S GO EXPLORING!*

*PLEASE NOTE: ALL TRAVEL IS AT YOUR OWN RISK. INTREPID EXPLORERS INC. OFFERS NO GUARANTEES OF SAFE RETURN OR RESCUE FROM DARK DUNGEONS, ABANDONED TOMBS OR FURIOUS GUARDS.

TIMELINE OF YOUR JOURNEYS

On your adventure through history, you're going to be travelling back to lots of different times and places. To help you make sense of where and when you are, here is a timeline for your travels. It won't help you return home if you get lost, but at least you'll know how many thousands of years it'll be before you need to be back in school.

1. THE GREAT PYRAMID OF GIZA

JOURNEY DATE: 2000 BCE

LOCATION: Egypt

2. THE HANGING GARDENS OF BABYLON

JOURNEY DATE: 580 BCE

LOCATION: Modern-day Iraq

3. THE STATUE OF ZEUS AT OLYMPIA

JOURNEY DATE: 396 BCE

LOCATION: Greece

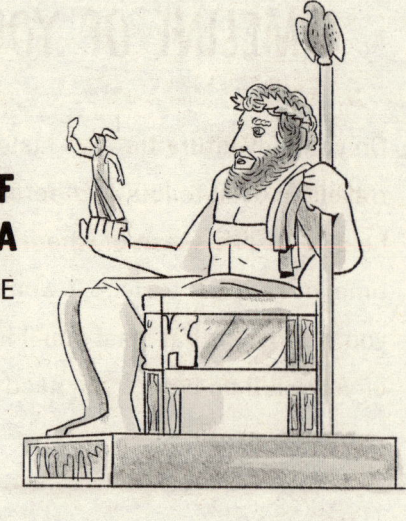

4. THE MAUSOLEUM OF HALICARNASSUS

JOURNEY DATE: 352 BCE

LOCATION: Modern-day Turkey

5. THE COLOSSUS OF RHODES

JOURNEY DATE: 250 BCE

LOCATION: Greece

6. THE LIGHTHOUSE OF ALEXANDRIA

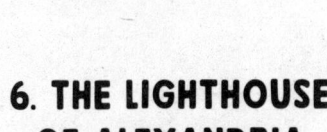

JOURNEY DATE: 30 BCE

LOCATION: Egypt

7. THE TEMPLE OF ARTEMIS AT EPHESUS

JOURNEY DATE: 120 CE

LOCATION: Modern-day Turkey

IMPORTANT NOTE FROM THE EDITOR

This is a non-fiction book. In other words, it contains facts about the ancient world and what it was like in those times. But since we can't *actually* travel back in time (sorry to disappoint you), some parts of this book have to be imagined.

So, how do you know what's true and what isn't? Easy! Everything that you SEE on your adventure is real. The places you visit, the buildings you enter, the information your pilot shares with you and the historical events you witness – they are all based on things that really existed and that actually happened.

However, during your adventure, you're going to meet people from the past (the kind of friendly people who want to put you in a rat-infested dungeon, for example). The *conversations* you have and overhear are not real. They are conversations that *might* happen if you could actually travel back in time and talk to these people.

Does that make sense? Good! Then you're ready to go.

CHAPTER 1:
THE GREAT PYRAMID OF GIZA

FACTS AND FIGURES

Completed: 2600–2500 BCE
Height: 146.5 metres
Size: 230 metres on each side
Special feature: made of
2.3 million stone blocks
Time to build: at least 20 years

WELCOME TO ANCIENT EGYPT!

The Great Pyramid of Giza was built in Egypt around 2600–2500 BCE. The kingdom of Egypt in northeast Africa was one of the oldest civilizations in history. While people in most parts of the world were still living in simple shelters or caves and hunting wild animals for food (yes, I know that sounds fun, but remember that wild animals tend to fight back), the Egyptians were living in mud-brick houses with bedrooms, bathrooms and stairs, building grand cities, growing crops on farms and inventing cool stuff like paper, make-up and toothpaste. They also created a written language called hieroglyphics – a system that used a series of symbols called hieroglyphs – and, unlike many other countries around the world at the time, they even had doctors that could perform surgery when people were sick.

A GOD FOR EVERY OCCASION

One thing that was very important to the Egyptians was their religion. They believed in many gods and goddesses, each of whom represented a different part of the natural world and helped them to understand important questions about their lives.

Why does the Sun rise and set each day? Because of a god called Ra who travels across the sky every day in a shining golden boat. What is the Moon? It's a god named Thoth who helps to separate day from night. What happens after we die? The god Osiris judges whether souls can live forever in the underworld – a paradise with beautiful rivers, fields and flowers.

These are just a few examples. In fact, the Egyptians believed in hundreds of gods and goddesses – they had one for pretty much every occasion. The god Sepa protected people from snake bites; Iat helped mothers to nurse their children; Ash provided a safe place for travellers in the desert; Ihy gave people music; and Dua, presumably because the other deities didn't like him much, was the god of . . . toilets. It's best not to think about when the Egyptians might have prayed to him.

'I WANT TO BE A GOD TOO!'

Egypt was a big country with lots of people, and it needed a powerful person in charge. The ruler of Egypt was called the pharaoh, and he wasn't just the king – he was also worshipped as a god. His job was to keep order in the world and make sure that Egypt remained strong and rich.

Being seen as a god gave the pharaoh great power.

People felt they had to do everything he told them, because disobeying the pharaoh was like insulting the gods. As long as life was peaceful and people had enough food to eat, the pharaoh could do pretty much anything he wanted.

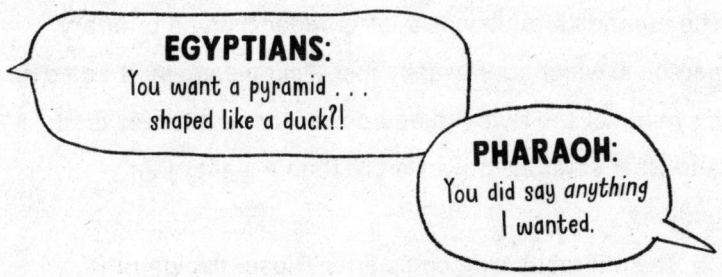

EGYPTIANS:
You want a pyramid . . . shaped like a duck?!

PHARAOH:
You did say *anything* I wanted.

THE FIRST BIG POINTY BUILDING

The pharaohs had a lot of responsibility defending their kingdom and all the people who lived there. So naturally they spent their time doing what you would expect any hardworking kings to do: they built huge pointy buildings in the desert.

The first pyramid was constructed by a pharaoh named Djoser in about 2650 BCE. Known as the Step Pyramid, it was sixty-two metres high, which is about the same height as twelve adult male giraffes stood on top of each other. It wasn't smooth on the outside like the later pyramids, but had six jutting layers, or steps, hence the name.

So, why did Djoser build it? Well, first of all, *he* didn't build it. Other people did. That was the advantage of being king. And it was designed to be his tomb – the place his body would be kept after he died. Pharaohs also liked to be buried alongside the belongings they might need in the underworld – some even had treasure with them. The pharaoh's tomb was a lot grander than an ordinary person's, which was usually just a simple grave. It acted as a symbol of their wealth and power long after they died. And what screams power more than a giant, pointy building?

The pharaohs who came after Djoser decided they wanted pyramids for their tombs too, and theirs had to be *even bigger*. The biggest pyramid of them all was built by Pharaoh Khufu around 2600–2500 BCE: the Great Pyramid of Giza. And that's where we're going now!

SURVIVE IN TIME

Right, did you get all that? Good, because it's time to start exploring. Step into my time machine and don't forget to wipe your feet. I've just had a new carpet laid and I don't want you trailing mud on it.

We're going to 2000 BCE, around 500 years after the Great Pyramid was completed. Your mission is to find your way into the pyramid and discover the chamber where the pharaoh was buried. Inside, there should be a stone coffin known as a sarcophagus. You never know, there might be treasure too!

As you explore, you'll have to make decisions about what to do and where to go. Choose carefully! The wrong option might land you in trouble. It's going to be hot in the Egyptian desert too, and there'll be lots of poisonous snakes and scorpions. But don't worry – if you really get stuck, I'm giving you a special watch that will transport you straight back to the time machine. You won't complete your mission, but at least you'll escape with your life. (And you can always start again and try to learn from your mistakes.)

Here is some other equipment you might need: a magnetic compass, a wooden torch and matches, and sticky climbing pads for your hands and feet, invented and patented by Intrepid Explorers Inc. Good luck. And if I never see you again, it's been nice knowing you!

***

It's hard to describe the sensation of travelling in a time machine. It's like riding a high-speed train through the countryside – except instead of green fields and hedges flashing past the window, there are swirling patterns and strange lights. Also, every now and then it turns upside down. And sometimes shoots straight up like a rocket. Occasionally it spins round and round for no good reason. Your stomach does somersaults and feels like it could fall out of your bottom at any minute.

Finally the machine makes a surprisingly gentle landing. You step out, extremely sick and dizzy, into the Egyptian desert. Behind you in the distance is a wide river – the great River Nile that meanders through the whole of Egypt. It glistens in the bright sunshine.

Talking of sunshine, it is *boiling* hot in the desert. You don't see any scorpions or snakes as you trudge forward all by yourself, which is a good start. But there's sweat pouring down your face and your shirt is sticking to your body like a wet cloth. You look a bit horrible, to be honest, and you don't smell that great either. It's probably good no one is around to see you.

At last, after walking for what feels like weeks, you finally see it in front of you – the Great Pyramid. In the present day, the pyramid is a sandy yellow colour, and the stone blocks are uneven and chipped. But here in 2000 BCE, the pyramid is covered by a layer of smooth, white stone. It gleams in the sun like a giant mirror. Incredible!

You get closer, panting for breath. From a distance, the structure had looked huge. But now you're standing next to it, it's bigger than huge. It's . . . what's a word that means bigger than huge? Huge-assive? Huge-ormous? Huge-opotamus? You don't even come up to the top of the first layer of stones, and above you there are 200 more layers rising high into the air. You want to go inside. But how do you get in? There's no sign of an opening anywhere. It's time for you to make your first decision!

OPTION 1:
WALK ROUND THE PYRAMID TO LOOK FOR AN ENTRANCE (PAGE 21)

OPTION 2:
CLIMB THE PYRAMID TO FIND A WAY IN (PAGE 23)

THE FIRST SMOOTH, POINTY BUILDING

In about 2600 BCE, a pharaoh named Sneferu came to the throne. Sneferu changed the way pyramids were designed. Up to this point, they had all been built as step pyramids, but Sneferu wanted his tomb to have smooth sides. He ordered a layer of polished white limestone to be placed around the entire outside of his pyramid so it would shine in the sun. His first two attempts were unsuccessful – one of the pyramids ended up bent and the other one fell down – but Sneferu was determined to get it right. Finally the third try was a success and the first smooth pyramid was complete. The builder of the Great Pyramid of Giza, Khufu, was Sneferu's son, and he copied this design for his own tomb.

YOU DECIDE TO WALK ROUND THE PYRAMID TO LOOK FOR AN ENTRANCE.

It's going to take a long time to get all the way round, because each side is 230 metres long. That's longer than two football fields!

Holding out your compass, you notice something interesting as you walk. Each side faces an exact direction: north, south, east and west. Since the Egyptians didn't have compasses like the one you're carrying, they used their knowledge of the stars and constellations to tell them the direction they were heading. For example, they knew a star called Thuban lined up with the North Pole, so that told them where north was.

Now, *where* is that entrance?

Good job there's no one around – I STINK!

You examine the base of the pyramid for signs of a door, but all you can see is a never-ending expanse of white limestone. It's not surprising the entrance is hard to find. The whole point of a tomb was that it would keep the king's body safe. They didn't want people breaking in, especially not sneaky children from the future who shouldn't even be there.

You're getting very tired, and the sun reflecting off the white stone is making you even hotter. You look like you've taken a bath in your own sweat. Gross. Eventually you get back to exactly the same place where you started. Well, that was pointless.

Now what?

OPTION 1:
CLIMB THE PYRAMID
TO FIND A WAY IN
(PAGE 23)

OPTION 2:
EXPLORE THE
SURROUNDING AREA
(PAGE 26)

YOU DECIDE TO CLIMB THE PYRAMID TO FIND A WAY IN.

This *must* be the right move. Why else would the pilot have given you sticky climbing pads? But it's no easy task. The layer of white limestone covering the structure is smooth, and even with your special pads, your hands and feet keep slipping as you pull yourself up. More than once, you think you're going to fall, and the higher you get, the scarier it becomes.

This is not a good time to realize you're frightened of heights. Your knees are wobbling like jelly, and you have to remind yourself NOT TO LOOK DOWN.

You haven't found any sign of the entrance, so you keep going higher and higher. Past halfway, beyond three-quarters, until finally – incredibly – you reach the very top. You stop to take some deep breaths. You're so tired you think you're going to faint, which wouldn't be a good idea when you're 146 and a half metres up in the air.

Slowly and carefully you turn round to take in the view. Wow! It looks like the whole of Egypt is spread out below you! There are two more pyramids, both smaller than the Great Pyramid, running in a diagonal line away from you. They were built by Khufu's son and grandson. There are large temples too, built for worshipping the dead pharaohs, and then, in the distance, next to the glistening waters of the River Nile, is the royal capital city of Memphis. You see sandy-coloured buildings surrounded by a high wall and a large gate.

The view made the perilous climb worth it. Unfortunately you didn't find an entrance. You could try climbing up one of the other sides, but that seems like an awful lot of hard work. Maybe it's time to try something different.

OPTION 1:
WALK ROUND THE PYRAMID TO LOOK FOR AN ENTRANCE (PAGE 21)

OPTION 2:
EXPLORE THE SURROUNDING AREA (PAGE 26)

HOW TO BUILD A PYRAMID

The Great Pyramid of Giza was made up of 2.3 million blocks of stone, with each stone weighing between two and eighty tonnes. Eighty tonnes is the same weight as fifteen elephants or, if you prefer, 20,000 cats. It took at least twenty years to build and required the labour of up to 40,000 workers at a time. For a long time, it was thought the workers were slaves. How else could you get people to work so hard on something so difficult? But now we know this wasn't the case. The pyramids were built by workers who were paid a salary. Often this salary came in the form of the Egyptians' favourite drink – beer!

The great blocks were made of slabs of limestone, which workers dragged across the sand on wooden sledges. Today we have modern machinery, such as cranes, to lift heavy materials. But how did they lift them in ancient Egypt? We think they used a lever system. The workers would insert a long pole with a flat end under one side of the block. By pushing down on the pole, they could lift up that side. Once it was in the air, they would pack sand underneath to keep it raised. Then they would move the pole to the other side of the block and repeat the process. Doing this exhausting work over and over allowed them to lift the stones higher and higher.

YOU DECIDE TO EXPLORE THE SURROUNDING AREA.

There are two smaller pyramids near Khufu's tomb, belonging to his son and grandson. But something in a different direction catches your eye. An enormous statue carved from stone. It looks like a lion lying on the ground with its paws out . . . but with a giant human head.

It's the Great Sphinx.

In the modern day, the Sphinx is the sandy colour of the rock it's carved from, but here in 2000 BCE it is painted with bright colours. The face is red and there are blue and gold patterns on its body. It's breathtaking! It was probably built by Khufu's son, Khafre. Khafre's pyramid might not have been quite as big as his father's, but he made up for it by putting his face on the body of a massive lion.

You walk around the Sphinx in awe, but the further you get from the Great Pyramid, the clearer it becomes that this isn't going to help you complete your mission.

You head back towards the pyramid. As you walk round to its north side, you suddenly notice something. Above your head, there appears to be a tiny gap in the stone. Could it be a door? It's about seventeen or eighteen metres up, so you whip out the sticky climbing pads the pilot provided.

Step by step, you climb the smooth, slippery stone until you finally reach the gap. You lean forward and poke your head through. It's an opening!

You shuffle through the small space, bending low so you don't bang your head. You're inside the pyramid now, and one step closer to finding where the pharaoh is buried!

There's a passage leading downwards. Using the shaft of sunlight shining through the opening to guide you, you crawl forward. Soon you come to a kind of crossroads. You can continue on your passage, which seems to be sloping down, or you can take another passage leading upward. Which one do you choose?

OPTION 1:
KEEP GOING DOWN THE
SAME PASSAGE
(PAGE 29)

OPTION 2:
TAKE THE PASSAGE
LEADING UPWARD
(PAGE 31)

THE AFTERLIFE

The pharaoh's tomb was very important, since the Egyptians believed a person's body should be preserved as fully as possible for life after death. Tombs protected pharaohs and queens from animals and robbers, and allowed them to be buried with the things they would need in the next life, such as furniture, pots, jewellery and their favourite snacks. After the workers placed the pharaoh's body in the tomb, they sealed the pyramid up with heavy stone blocks.

PHARAOH:
Right, we're going to need crisps, marshmallows, chocolates, peanut butter, popcorn, ice cream and Jaffa Cakes in my tomb.

SCRIBE:
I don't think there's a hieroglyph for Jaffa Cakes.

YOU DECIDE TO KEEP GOING DOWN THE SAME PASSAGE.

For a few more metres, the sunlight allows you to see where you're going, but gradually it gets darker and darker. What can you do? You don't have a flashlight. Then you remember the wooden torch and matches the pilot gave you. You've never lit a torch before, but how hard can it be? You strike a match and hold it to the end of the torch. The torch flares up into a bright flame and immediately sets fire to your hair. Whoops!

Who needs a flashlight?

By the light of your blazing head, you can see the passage stretches down a long way into the darkness. Quickly you pat down your hair until the fire is extinguished and continue to walk forward, keeping your head low.

The torch makes ghostly shadows on the walls around you and provides just enough light for you to see where you're putting your feet. You're walking on dusty stone and the walls are bare. The temperature drops and the sweat on your face starts to dry.

For almost a hundred metres you follow the passage, until suddenly you come to a room. Is it the pharaoh's burial chamber? Excitedly you step inside and swing the torch around you. But you're disappointed. It seems like the room wasn't finished. There's nothing inside but bare rock.

You've reached a dead end.

OPTION 1:
RETRACE YOUR STEPS AND TAKE THE PASSAGE LEADING UPWARD (PAGE 31)

OPTION 2:
ACTIVATE YOUR SPECIAL WATCH (PAGE 40)

YOU DECIDE TO TAKE THE PASSAGE LEADING UPWARD.

You know that all the tunnels in the pyramid were closed up with heavy stones after the pharaoh was placed inside. So why is this one open? Has someone been here before you?

Or did the pharaoh's mummy come back to life and move this stone itself? That happens all the time in movies, and it never ends well.

You've lit the wooden torch the pilot gave you and you grip it tightly in one hand while pressing your other hand against the wall. It's hard work walking up the slope. After about forty metres, the passage levels off, which allows you to move more quickly.

A shiver of anticipation runs up your spine. Surely this leads to where the pharaoh is buried?! Perhaps you'll find some treasure too. You wonder what you'll do with all the gold, and decide you'll make a house built entirely of chocolate and slowly eat your way from the living room to the bathroom.

No such luck. When you reach the end, you find an empty room known as the Queen's Chamber. It's very eerie inside the bare room, and the longer you don't see the pharaoh's coffin, the more nervous you become. Where is he?

Flashes of horror films come to mind, with images of terrifying mummies chasing people down. You gulp. Maybe this was a bad idea. Retracing your steps, you notice one more passage, but it looks very dark. Do you want to take the risk?

OPTION 1:
TAKE THE DARK PASSAGE (PAGE 34)

OPTION 2:
FIND YOUR WAY BACK TO THE ENTRANCE (PAGE 38)

HOW TO MAKE A MUMMY

You've probably seen mummies in pictures, movies or even museums. They're the scary-looking bodies all wrapped up in white bandages. The idea behind mummies was to preserve the body for living again in the afterlife.

To mummify someone, the Egyptians removed all the moisture from the body, leaving only a dried form that would not easily decay. It was a difficult process that only the rich could afford, and for someone like a pharaoh it was considered very important. Here's how it was done:

1. Using a small hook, pull the brain out through the nostrils and throw away. (The Egyptians didn't think the brain was important.)

2. Remove the body's internal organs — such as the heart, lungs, stomach and liver — and let them dry.

3. Keep most of the organs in jars but put the heart back inside the body. (Egyptians believed a person's mind was in their heart.)

4. Cover the body with salt for seventy days to get rid of all the moisture.

5. Fill the body with sand and wrap it in bandages.

6. Place the body in a sarcophagus and hope it doesn't come alive again. (Unlikely considering what happened in steps 1–5, but you never know.)

YOU DECIDE TO TAKE THE DARK PASSAGE.

The entrance has three huge granite stones lying on their sides. They must have previously been used to block the passage, but they've now been moved. You shudder – if it was the pharaoh's undead mummy that did that, it must be extremely strong.

You climb over them and find yourself in a much bigger passage. The ceiling is more than eight metres high. You're in what's called the Grand Gallery, and this time you feel sure you're heading in the right direction. You touch the smooth limestone walls as you walk along, until finally you reach a large chamber at the end.

You shine the torch forward and, near the far wall, you see a large object. Is that . . .?

Yes, it's a sarcophagus!

In a state of nervous excitement, you move forward to take a look. You've never seen a real mummy before, and if there's treasure to be found, it's going to be here. You can almost taste that chocolate house.

You reach the sarcophagus and jump in shock when you see that the lid has been pushed to the floor. Has the pharaoh really awoken?! You peer over the edge of the coffin and look inside.

It's empty.

Suddenly you hear a noise, a kind of scratching above you.

It sounds like it might be a rat, but equally it could be Khufu's mummy trying to catch a rat.

Because until you came, rats were the only thing in the pyramid to eat.

You decide not to find out which it is. You abandon the empty sarcophagus and rush out of the chamber. But at this vital moment, the torch goes out. In the darkness, you feel your way along the cold walls, trying not to trip as you hastily make your escape. You soon realize you're in a passage you haven't been in before. It's much narrower and lower than the others, and you have to duck down and crawl on your hands and knees. Without your torch, it's completely black, and you can't even see your fingers as they scramble around in front of you.

Where is the passage leading? It seems to be going deeper into the pyramid, which is not what you want at all.

But it's too small for you to turn around in. The narrow walls seem to be closing in on you and you can't even activate your watch, as it's impossible to see which buttons to press in the darkness!

As panic starts to rise, the passage suddenly comes to an end and you find yourself in one a little more spacious. Phew.

You turn your head to the left and, with a cry of delight, catch sight of a small pinprick of light. You go up towards it as quickly as you can, and, at last, emerge into the bright sunshine of the Egyptian desert. Miraculously you had found yourself in the escape tunnel the workers used to leave the pyramid after they'd blocked off all the openings.

You're free!

OPTION 1:
WALK BACK THROUGH THE DESERT TO THE TIME MACHINE (PAGE 39)

OPTION 2:
HEAD BACK INTO THE PYRAMID AND KEEP LOOKING FOR TREASURE (PAGE 37)

THIS WASN'T THE RIGHT DECISION, I'M AFRAID.

You end up getting completely lost and never find your way back out. But don't worry! The following letter will be provided to anyone interested in your whereabouts:

Dear parent, guardian, teacher or interested person,

It is with great regret that we inform you of the loss of [insert name here] in the Great Pyramid of Giza. It appears they failed to return to the transport vehicle by the scheduled time. Although at this point it is difficult to know where (or when) they are, we can assure you we are doing everything in our power to find them.

Please be aware that [insert name here] was clearly warned of the risks involved with their journey. The company cannot, therefore, take any financial responsibility for their disappearance.

Yours sincerely,

Intrepid Explorers Inc.

Think you could do better next time?
Go back and start again on page 17!

YOU DECIDE TO FIND YOUR WAY BACK TO THE ENTRANCE.

You retrace your steps and make your way back through the passages, praying that you don't get caught by a roaming, undead mummy. In your panic, you accidentally knock your torch against the wall. It goes out, plunging you into complete darkness. You rummage in your pockets for the matches, but you can't find them anywhere. They must have fallen out of your pocket. Oh no!

You speedily make your way down another passage and then another, the fear rising inside of you. You can't see a single thing and have no idea if you're heading towards the entrance or deeper into the pyramid.

Your mind fills with the thought of Khufu's mummy. Which part of your body will he eat first? Your arms? Your legs? Or will he go straight for your brain? Is your brain even big enough to satisfy him?

Suddenly you realize it's not quite as dark as before. In the distance, there's a shaft of light shining into the passage. The entrance! Somehow you managed to make it back to where you started. You crawl out into the sunshine, exhausted. You're incredibly relieved to have made it out safely, but on the downside you still haven't found the pharaoh's burial chamber. You have another decision to make.

OPTION 1:
ENTER THE PYRAMID
AND START AGAIN
(PAGE 23)

OPTION 2:
ACTIVATE YOUR
SPECIAL WATCH
(PAGE 40)

CONGRATULATIONS! YOU COMPLETED YOUR MISSION!

You reached Khufu's burial chamber and made it out of the Great Pyramid alive. It's a shame you didn't find any treasure, but it wasn't your fault. Around 400 years after the pyramid was built, Egypt suffered a period of chaos when a lack of rain meant there wasn't enough water to grow crops to feed everyone. The people blamed the pharaohs, and the kings lost all their power.

Furious thieves broke into the pyramids in Giza and stole everything inside, including Khufu's body – which has never been found. That's why all the stones had been removed from the tunnels. It wasn't the king's undead mummy after all.

You find the pilot waiting for you outside the time machine.

'How was your trip?' he asks. 'Did you find any treasure?'

'No. I can't even afford to buy a chocolate bar, never mind build a chocolate house,' you complain. 'Can we go now?'

'Sure. But only after you take a shower. You smell horrible.'

Why couldn't I have had this map at the start?

YOU DECIDE TO ACTIVATE YOUR SPECIAL WATCH.

Unfortunately you didn't manage to complete your mission and find the pharaoh's burial chamber. But at least you're still alive. That's better than nothing.

'Are you ready to go?' the pilot asks, as he opens the door of the time machine.

'Yes, I think so,' you answer. 'Pyramids are hard places to explore.'

He agrees. 'Never mind, perhaps you'll have better luck at our next destination.'

Think you could do better next time?
Go back and start again on page 17!

CHAPTER 2:
THE HANGING GARDENS OF BABYLON

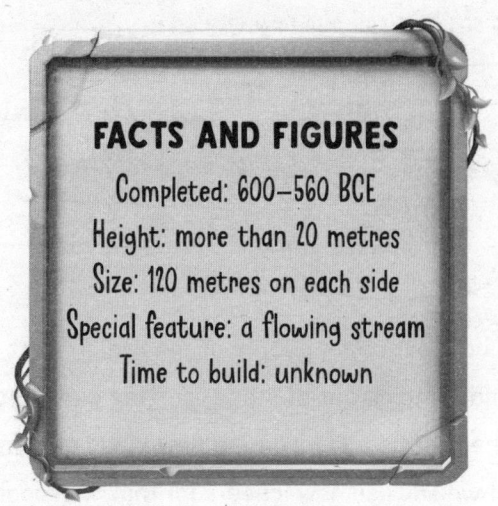

FACTS AND FIGURES

Completed: 600–560 BCE

Height: more than 20 metres

Size: 120 metres on each side

Special feature: a flowing stream

Time to build: unknown

WELCOME TO MESOPOTAMIA!

People haven't always lived together in big cities, which means ancient children didn't understand the pain of being stuck with their parents in the car when they're trying to find a parking space in a busy city centre. The first large cities were founded in Mesopotamia (now modern-day Iraq). It was a rich and prosperous land, thanks to two great rivers: the Tigris and the Euphrates, which flowed through the region and ensured fertile soil for farming.

The biggest Mesopotamian cities included Kish, Akkad,

Babylon and, my personal favourite, Ur, which sounds like people were just hesitating about what to call it.

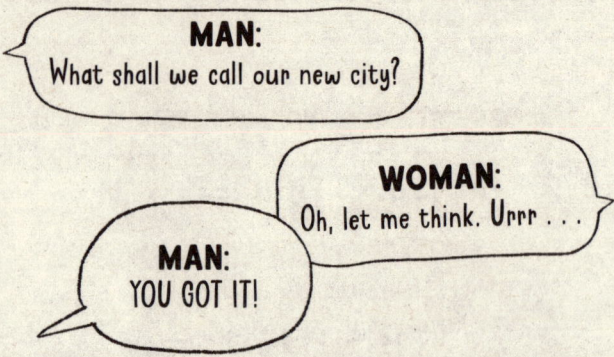

MAN:
What shall we call our new city?

WOMAN:
Oh, let me think. Urrr . . .

MAN:
YOU GOT IT!

Thousands of years ago, people of the region were building palaces and temples out of stone, digging canals to bring water to their farms and inventing new kinds of complicated maths that we still use now (cheers for that, Mesopotamians). They were also the first people to start measuring time in units of sixty minutes and seconds, just like we do today.

TOUGHEST KID ON THE BLOCK

Things were not always peaceful in Mesopotamia. Each city had its own king, and sometimes an ambitious ruler would decide he wanted to take over another city or two, or ten, or twenty. This led to wars, which in those days were fought by soldiers carrying swords and shields made of bronze (the first metal that humans learned how to mould and shape).

The first conqueror of ancient Mesopotamia was called Sargon the Great, which is undoubtedly the best name for a conqueror ever. He sounds like an intergalactic villain who rules over the entire universe. In reality he forged an empire from his home city of Akkad that stretched over parts of what is now Iraq, Iran and Syria. (Not quite the entire universe, but still pretty impressive.)

The second conqueror was Hammurabi of Babylon. Babylon was a great city built over the Euphrates, which flowed right through it. From about 1792 BCE, Hammurabi carved out another huge empire and made Babylon the most powerful kingdom in the region.

KING NEBUCHADNEZZAR OF BAAAAAAABYLON

The frequent wars in Mesopotamia meant that Babylon didn't remain the most powerful city for very long. But in about 605 BCE they got a new king who was determined to get it to the top again. His name was Nebuchadnezzar II (pronounced *Neh-bu-kuhd-neh-zer*), and he did several interesting things as king: he made a great empire larger than Hammurabi's; he built the Hanging Gardens of Babylon; and he thought he was a goat. Let's talk about the goat thing first.

According to a Bible story, at some point during his

reign, Nebuchadnezzar forgot he was ruler of the most powerful kingdom in Mesopotamia and began to think he was a goat, or possibly a cow (people didn't like to ask). He grew his hair long, walked on his hands and knees, drank water from a river and ate grass from the fields. This went on for seven years, which is a long time considering that grass is, frankly, very hard for humans to digest. When he eventually snapped out of it, he continued his work as one of the greatest rulers of the ancient world.

AN ANCIENT MYSTERY

The Hanging Gardens of Babylon are the most mysterious of all of the Seven Wonders of the Ancient World, because archaeologists haven't been able to find any evidence that they really existed. The Babylonians didn't mention them in any surviving records, and some historians even think they weren't in Babylon at all, but a different city called Nineveh. The ancient Greeks, however, believed the gardens were in Babylon and that they were built after around 600 BCE by Nebuchadnezzar II. They described the gardens based on stories they heard.

The Greeks said Nebuchadnezzar built the wonder as a gift for his wife, Queen Amytis. Before she was a queen, Amytis was a beautiful princess from a mountainous kingdom called Media. She loved her husband but didn't like living in Babylon, which was dusty and flat compared to her own land. Nebuchadnezzar wanted to do something to make his wife feel at home, so he had a garden constructed next to his palace that would look like the hills of her homeland. He planted trees and flowers from Media and made a cascade of water that flowed down from the top like a mountain stream. This stream is another mystery about the Hanging Gardens. Babylon was in a dry region where it very rarely rained, so how did they get water to keep flowing down over the garden?

It looks like we have some investigating to do.

SURVIVE IN TIME

Let's go exploring! We're going to travel back to 580 BCE, just after the gardens were built. Your mission this time is to find the Hanging Gardens of Babylon and see how they made that mysterious stream of water.

Again, you'll be on your own once you get there and will have to make decisions as you go along. But be careful! If the Babylonians catch you snooping around, they might think you're a spy from a rival city. Spying was common in the dangerous world of ancient Mesopotamia, and I imagine the penalty would be getting thrown off the city walls or something fun like that.

Here is your special watch to transport you back to the time machine if you're in real trouble. I'm also giving you some clothes so you can blend in, and an AI-powered translation device in case you have to talk to someone.

***

This time, you're prepared for the violent twisting, diving, spinning and looping of the time machine and manage to make it through the journey without reaching for the sick bag. The pilot lands just outside the city of Babylon.

As you step out of the door, you're greeted by the fierce heat of the sun and the strong smell of dusty earth. A crowd of men and women, dressed in loose, flowing garments of linen and wool, are bustling about in small groups, chatting together in a language you've never heard before. They're carrying large, woven baskets full of fruit, bread and vegetables they plan to sell inside the city. Some lead animals on ropes – sheep, goats and a few majestic horses, their coats gleaming.

You've changed into your local dress – a brown woollen robe with a pair of sandals to protect your feet. You follow the crowd towards the main gate of the city, letting out a gasp as you see the size of it. It's higher than a three-storey building and as thick as the length of a car. It's called the Gate of Ishtar, and it's made from glazed blue and gold bricks and decorated with images of dragons and bulls. It's magnificent!

On either side of the gate are massive walls made of hard mud bricks. You can make out soldiers standing guard on the top, scanning the horizon for signs of enemy invaders.

There are steps inside the Gate of Ishtar leading to the top of the wall, and you wonder about climbing them to get a good view of the city. You'll have to dodge the soldiers if you go up, but it will be worth it if you can see where the Hanging Gardens are located.

OPTION 1:
CLIMB TO THE TOP OF THE WALL (PAGE 49)

OPTION 2:
PASS THROUGH THE GATE OF ISHTAR (PAGE 51)

AN EYE FOR AN EYE AND A TOOTH FOR A TOOTH

Babylon is famous for being one of the first kingdoms in history to write down its laws. They were carved into a big piece of stone by King Hammurabi, who reigned from about 1792 to 1750 BCE. The laws were based on the idea of 'an eye for an eye and a tooth for a tooth'. In other words, if you did something bad to someone, the same thing would be done to you. This is what the law said: 'If a man puts out the eye of another man, his eye will be put out. If he breaks another man's bone, his bone will be broken. If he takes out the tooth of another man, his tooth will be taken out.'

YOU DECIDE TO CLIMB TO THE TOP OF THE WALL.

You're nervous as you climb the steps, remembering the pilot's warning about what the Babylonians might do to enemy spies. Luckily when you reach the top, the guards are all facing the other way.

You can hardly believe it when you step on to the wall. It's so wide! Six people could walk side by side without falling off. In fact, at this time, the wall is the largest in the ancient world and Babylon is the biggest city.

It's very hot and the air is dusty and dry. You look out beyond the city, which is situated on a wide, expansive plain. The land is very flat, but there's one feature that stands out: a large brown river flowing directly into the city. This is the river Euphrates, the source of Babylon's strength. Without the river,

I don't fancy getting thrown from this wall.

there would be no water for drinking or growing food. You can see fields spreading out from the banks where farmers are busy cultivating crops of wheat and barley. You can also see bushes and trees where grapes, olives and dates are growing. The land looks rich and full of life.

'Hey, who are you? What are you doing up here?'

Your AI translator picks up an angry voice to your left. A guard is coming towards you with an enormous spear! You have one second to decide what to do: dash back down the steps and pass through the gate or stand your ground.

OPTION 1:
PASS THROUGH THE
GATE OF ISHTAR
(PAGE 51)

OPTION 2:
TRY TO PUSH PAST THE
GUARD (PAGE 55)

YOU DECIDE TO PASS THROUGH THE GATE OF ISHTAR.
You find yourself on a wide road paved with stone
called the Processional Way. The walls on each side
are decorated with more than a hundred images of
lions, bulls and dragons fashioned from glazed blue and
gold bricks, like those on the gate. The creatures appear
to be walking beside you as you move along, and it's
impressive and scary at the same time. The lions
symbolize Ishtar, the Babylonian goddess of love
and war.

The Processional Way takes you into the hustle and
bustle of the city. The streets here are much narrower,
and they're no longer made of stone but rather hard
brown earth. On either side are small houses packed
closely together. You see a family eating a meal of bread
and fruit on the flat roof of their home. This is where
Babylonians spend a lot of their time, because there's
more light on the roof and they can enjoy a small breeze
passing through the hot, dry air.

You notice someone appear in the doorway of their
house. They have a pile of rubbish in their hands, which
they throw out into the street. Well, half of it lands over
you, actually. You're wondering if the pilot is going to
complain about how you smell again, when everybody
suddenly jumps to the side of the road. You get out of

the way just in time as a troop of soldiers march past carrying spears and shields. Where are they going?

OPTION 1:
FOLLOW THE SOLDIERS (PAGE 53)

OPTION 2:
CONTINUE EXPLORING THE CITY (PAGE 57)

YOU DECIDE TO FOLLOW THE SOLDIERS.

They're wearing armour and helmets shaped like a cone, and each one has a spear and shield as well as a sword swinging at his belt. You keep a safe distance as you follow them through the narrow streets.

They take you over a wide bridge across the Euphrates. In front of you is a walled enclosure. Just outside it, you see a huge structure rising almost a hundred metres into the air. It looks a bit like the Step Pyramid built by Pharaoh Djoser, but there are stairs so you can climb up to each layer. This is a famous temple called Etemananki, also known as the Tower of Babel. The Babylonians – who, like the Egyptians, had lots of gods – built it to worship their most important god, Marduk.

The soldiers head to a gate in the walled enclosure, which is decorated with the same sort of images you saw on the Gate of Ishtar and the Processional Way. Could the enclosure contain Nebuchadnezzar's palace, where the Hanging Gardens are supposed to be? There are guards standing at the gate, so it'd be too dangerous to follow the soldiers through. You could try climbing over the wall, or continue exploring the city to find a safer way in.

OPTION 1:
CONTINUE EXPLORING
THE CITY (PAGE 57)

OPTION 2:
CLIMB OVER THE WALL
(PAGE 60)

THE TOWER OF BABEL

Etemananki, or the Tower of Babel, was a real temple built for Marduk, but there's also a legend about it in the Bible. You know how at school they make you learn a foreign language like French or Spanish, and you think: *Wouldn't it be easier if everyone in the world all spoke the same language?* We'd call it Earthish or Globeish. It wouldn't have any weird spellings like 'rhythm', 'jeopardy' or 'conscience', and nobody would use long words just to show off how sagacious they are. (See what I did there?) Well, you can blame the Tower of Babel. According to the Bible, the Babylonians decided to build a tower in their city that was so high it would reach all the way to the heavens. But God felt this would make them too smug. To stop their plan, he mixed up the languages of the workers so they couldn't understand each other. Unable to communicate, the workers made lots of mistakes and the Tower of Babel was never completed. The Bible says this is why there are so many different languages across the world today.

Hey, be careful of that rock! It's going to land on your head!

Excusez-moi, je ne compr– Ow!

YOU DECIDE TO TRY TO PUSH PAST THE GUARD.

Are you sure about this? This is a soldier we're talking about, a man trained to fight professionally. You, on the other hand, are a child from the twenty-first century with spindly arms and legs and a fear of giant spears.

As you try to get past him, he grabs you by the wrist and drags you off. Before you know it, you're being hauled down stone steps into a dungeon. Is this better than being thrown from the walls of the city? That remains to be seen.

The dungeon isn't a nice place to be – it's even worse than that time your parents made you go shopping with them in IKEA. It's dark and cold, with rough, damp walls. It smells musty and earthy, like wet socks. Thick wooden doors line the sides of the corridor, and you hear sad moans from the prisoners locked behind them.

The guard opens one of the doors with a large iron key and pushes you through it. You land on the hard stone floor with a thump. All you can see in the dim light are four bare stone walls. There's no window, bed, chair, table or toilet. You start to wish you were back in IKEA. The one thing it did have was furniture.

The guard slams the heavy door shut.

OPTION 1:
WAIT FOR THE GUARD TO COME BACK (PAGE 62)

OPTION 2:
ACTIVATE YOUR SPECIAL WATCH (PAGE 65)

TOP SECRET!

The Babylonians probably think you're a spy, which is not good news for you. Spying was an important part of warfare in ancient Mesopotamia, and was a common way for kings to try to get secret information about their enemies. There was even a tribe called the Zalmaqum who specialized in sneaking into cities and sending reports back home. It was said they had to be paid lots of money for their work.

Archaeologists discovered a clay tablet (which is what the Mesopotamians used instead of paper) from about 1813 BCE. It was marked SECRET. It was an order from a king to arrest a man who was plotting against him.

YOU DECIDE TO CONTINUE EXPLORING THE CITY.

You make your way through narrow streets until eventually you reach a marketplace with stalls selling bread, fish, vegetables, fruit and herbs. The shopkeepers are shouting out at passers-by, telling them what they're selling, while children play together on the ground with wooden dolls and toy soldiers. One woman is cooking at her stall, putting pieces of lamb and beetroot into a reddish stew. It smells delicious, but the pilot didn't give you any money to buy things.

At the next stall, a man is selling . . . what are those? They look like dried grasshoppers, but bigger. A sign next to them says they're locusts! A customer picks one up and pops it into his mouth, crunching the insect between his teeth. Maybe it doesn't taste as bad as it looks? Curious, you start to reach over.

'Oi! Thief! That child is trying to steal my delicious locusts!' the shopkeeper shouts. He tries to grab your hand.

Suddenly everyone has turned towards you, their faces angry.

'Get the little locust thief!'

You panic and start to run, darting under the stall and away from the shopkeeper's hand. Unfortunately your bottom catches the edge, and the stall topples over, spilling insects all over the floor.

'My beautiful locusts!' the shopkeeper cries. 'Catch that monstrous child!'

You keep running, swerving through the crowded marketplace. From behind, you hear the shopkeeper and his friends running after you. Your lungs feel like they're going to burst as you run faster than you've ever run before.

Somehow you make it out of the square and into the streets, dashing over a wide bridge across the Euphrates. Turning to look behind you to see if you're still being chased, you crash straight into a high wall with a thud. There's nowhere to run.

OPTION 1:
BEG FOR MERCY
(PAGE 62)

OPTION 2:
CLIMB OVER THE WALL
(PAGE 60)

HOW TO BE
A KID IN
BABYLON

Being a child in ancient Babylon wasn't like being a kid today. For instance, unless you were a rich noble, you didn't go to school. Sounds great, right? Well, no, because instead of school, you had to work, usually helping your family with their farm or craft. There was a bit of time to play though, and kids had simple toys like dolls, soldiers, boats, skipping ropes, spinning tops and slingshots. There were board games too. People in Mesopotamia invented a game similar to the modern game of draughts (or checkers), and they had six-sided dice made of bone or clay.

YOU DECIDE TO CLIMB OVER THE WALL.

It's not easy, but you manage to clamber up and swing
your legs over to the other side, landing inside a walled
enclosure. You drop down behind a bush and find yourself
in a spacious garden full of colourful flowers. In front of you
is a large and imposing building with thick walls decorated,
again, with blue and gold bricks. It looks like it was built
both as a fortress and a palace. Something else draws your
eye. Behind a long row of columns, there are tall trees that
appear to be growing in mid-air. You creep forward to take a
closer look, keeping your eye out for guards.

Now that you're nearer, you can see the trees are actually
planted on a series of square terraces. Each terrace is
standing on top of the other, the largest at the bottom and
the smallest at the top, in a kind of pyramid shape. There
are steps leading up to each one. Checking there's no one
around, you creep up the first set of steps. The trees are
rooted in deep soil beside beds of beautiful red, yellow and
purple flowers.

Three more levels stand above you, and as you look up,
you notice a stream of water dropping down from the
terrace above. It trickles through the soil to feed the trees
and flowers, before falling over the edge like a small
waterfall. This must be the flow of water Nebuchadnezzar
built to resemble the mountain streams of his wife's

homeland! You realize where you're standing – this is the Hanging Gardens of Babylon.

You remember the second part of your mission: to discover how the stream was made. But suddenly there's a noise – a startled shout from a woman. You spin round and see a dark-haired lady in a long dress of swirling purple-and-green patterns. She has gold jewellery round her neck and precious stones on her fingers. She looks beautiful! Is it Queen Amytis? You think about saying hello when another figure appears: a guard armed with a huge spear!

OPTION 1:
TRY TO PUSH PAST THE
GUARD (PAGE 55)

OPTION 2:
DASH UP TO THE NEXT
TERRACE (PAGE 63)

BAD MOVE.

It isn't long before you're grabbed by a guard. The Babylonians are very suspicious of strange children with weird, futuristic AI translators in their pockets. They're already debating which wall to throw you off. But it's OK! The following letter will be provided to anyone interested in your whereabouts:

Dear parent, guardian, teacher or interested person,

It is with great regret that we inform you of the loss of [insert name here] in the Hanging Gardens of Babylon. It appears they failed to return to the transport vehicle by the scheduled time. Although at this point it is difficult to know where (or when) they are, we can assure you we are doing everything in our power to find them.

Please be aware that [insert name here] was clearly warned of the risks involved with their journey. The company cannot, therefore, take any financial responsibility for their disappearance.

Yours sincerely,

Intrepid Explorers Inc.

Think you could do better next time?
Go back and start again on page 46!

YOU DECIDE TO DASH UP TO THE NEXT TERRACE.

The guard is too slow to react, and you make it up the first set of stairs before he even moves. Two more terraces remain above you, but you're determined to complete your mission and keep going to the top. Perhaps there'll be somewhere to hide there. From below, you hear the guard shouting for you to stop, his sword clinking against his armour as he runs.

You sprint to the top terrace, which is filled with the most beautiful flowers you've ever seen – dazzling pink and blue orchids that scent the air with a sweet fragrance. As you look around frantically for a hiding place, you notice a man working beside a pool of water. He sees you too, but you've no time to introduce yourself. You hear the clink of armour and duck behind a flowering bush.

'Have you seen a child come up here?' the guard demands sharply.

You hold your breath, praying that the man won't give you away.

'Yes! They jumped down there.'

Through the bush, you see the worker point down to the terrace below. The guard nods and runs off back the way he came. Relief floods through you. Slowly you emerge from your hiding place and look at the smiling man in grateful amazement.

You thank him profusely before taking a closer look at what he's doing. He's turning a wheel that's connected to a long chain. It has buckets of water hung from it at regular intervals. As the wheel turns, the chain pulls the buckets up towards the top terrace. When they reach the water pool, they tip over and deposit their contents into it. From the pool, the water trickles out into a stream that flows through the garden.

'There's a bigger pool at the bottom,' the man explains, noticing your quizzical expression. 'The buckets are filled from there and I bring them up to the top by turning the wheel. That's how the stream keeps flowing.'

'You must get very tired turning that wheel.'

'I really do!' the man answers with a grimace. 'That's why I didn't give you away to the guard. He never lets me rest!' He shrugs his shoulders as he continues to work. 'But it's OK, I guess. At least I have a nice view.'

That's an understatement. From this top terrace, the whole of Babylon and the wide Mesopotamian plain is spread out before you like a painting. There's also a pleasant breeze wafting through the air. You thank the worker again, wondering how you can repay his bravery and kindness. The only thing you can think of is to take over his work for a while so he can finally take a break. But what if the guard sees you?

OPTION 1:
TAKE OVER THE MAN'S
WORK (PAGE 62)

OPTION 2:
SNEAK BACK TO THE
TIME MACHINE
(PAGE 66)

YOU ACTIVATE YOUR SPECIAL WATCH AND RETURN TO THE TIME MACHINE.

Unfortunately you didn't manage to complete your mission of seeing the flowing waters in the Hanging Gardens of Babylon. The pilot greets you with a disapproving shake of his head.

'Your plan was to take on a Babylonian soldier? Really? You know the Babylonians conquered the whole of Mesopotamia, right?' he exclaims incredulously. 'Have you ever conquered the whole of Mesopotamia?'

'I suppose I haven't,' you admit.

He sighs heavily. 'All right, let's go. We're heading to ancient Greece next. Try not to start a war, please.'

feeling brave enough to give it another try?
Go back to page 46!

CONGRATULATIONS! YOU COMPLETED YOUR MISSION!

You visited the Hanging Gardens and discovered the secret of how they made the water flow through it. The pilot pats you on the back as you get into the time machine.

'Good work on reaching the Hanging Gardens without being thrown off the city walls. You're much better at this than a lot of my guests,' he says generously.

You give him a sideways glance. 'Er . . . thanks. How many of your guests have been thrown off the city walls?'

The pilot chuckles. 'Let's just say there's a reason I carry a scrubbing brush in the time machine. You know – for the splat.'

You shudder, and the pilot continues. 'But it's great you're still in one piece. You're going to love our next destination. We're going to the Olympic Games!'

CHAPTER 3:
THE STATUE OF ZEUS AT OLYMPIA

FACTS AND FIGURES

Completed: about 435 BCE

Height: 12.4 metres

Materials: gold, ivory, wood

Special feature: the artist
signed it

Time to build: 8 years

WELCOME TO OLYMPIA!

The next ancient wonder we're going to visit is the Statue of Zeus. It was a large and beautiful statue that looked so lifelike it seemed to be alive. The statue was located in Olympia in southern Greece. Olympia was famous for two great temples: one dedicated to Zeus (where the statue was kept) and the other to Hera. People travelled from all over Greece to worship at them.

But who were Zeus and Hera? They were the king and queen of the Greek gods. Like the Egyptians and Babylonians, the Greeks believed in lots of gods and goddesses. The twelve most important ones were known as the Olympian gods and were believed to live on top of Mount Olympus, a real mountain in north-eastern Greece. The group included Zeus and Hera; Poseidon, god of the sea; Athena, goddess of wisdom; Hestia, goddess of the home; Apollo, god of poetry and music; Aphrodite, goddess of love; and Ares, god of war.

VOMITED TO VICTORY!

The Greeks told many stories, known as myths, about their gods and goddesses. One is about how Zeus became king of the gods. The story says that before the Olympian gods ruled over Greece, there were twelve older gods known as Titans in charge. They were led by their cruel king, Cronus. Cronus was actually the father of six of the Olympian gods, but he'd heard a prophecy that one day his children would overthrow him. To prevent this happening, he swallowed each child when they were born. (I strongly recommend hiding this book from your parents so they don't get any funny ideas.)

Demeter (later goddess of the harvest), Hestia, Hera, Hades (later god of the underworld) and Poseidon all suffered this sticky fate. But when Zeus was born, his mother was determined that she would save at least one of her children. She hid him in a cave and gave Cronus a stone to swallow instead. Cronus, who wasn't the smartest evil god in the world, didn't notice the difference, and so Zeus secretly grew up.

When he was old enough to challenge his father, Zeus disguised himself as a servant and gave Cronus a special potion that made the king vomit up his swallowed children. Once they were over the whole ordeal of being thrown up, the kids joined together and took on Cronus and the Titans, eventually defeating them in a fierce ten-year war. Zeus imprisoned the defeated giants in an underground prison called Tartarus.

> **CRONUS**:
> If only I'd *chewed* my kids instead of just swallowing them!

HOW *NOT* TO FIND A WIFE

Along with the temples of Zeus and Hera, Olympia was also famous for being the site of the first Olympic Games. According to a Greek myth, the Olympics started with a test made by a king called Oenomaus (pronounced *E-no-ma-us*), who wanted to find a suitable husband for his beautiful daughter, Hippodamia. He organized a chariot race between himself and any man who wanted to marry his daughter. If the suitor won the race, he could marry Hippodamia; if he lost, he would forfeit his life.

Thirteen young men tried, but each lost the race, and then his life. Eventually a grandson of Zeus called Pelops stepped forward. Even Oenomaus couldn't beat the grandson of a god. Pelops won the race and married Hippodamia, becoming a great king. Legend says that he started the Olympic Games to celebrate his victory.

THE REAL OLYMPIC GAMES

Another, more likely, theory for where the Olympic Games comes from is a festival the Greeks held at Olympia in 776 BCE to honour Zeus. They held a running race to entertain the god in his temple. The race was called the *stadion*, which is where we get the word 'stadium' from. It was a sprint of nearly 200 metres and, at first, this race – which takes around twenty to thirty seconds – was the only event in the Olympic Games.

Over time, the Olympic Games grew larger, and included such events as chariot racing, boxing, wrestling, the long jump, the discus, the javelin and an anything-goes-fight called the *pankration* (which we'll learn more about later).

Unlike today, for most sports it was only men who were allowed to compete in the Olympics. Chariot racing was the one and only event in which women were allowed to join the fun, since it was the owner of the chariot rather than the driver who became the Olympic champion. The first woman to become a chariot-racing champion was a Spartan princess named Cynisca.

Now we've covered that, are you ready for the next stop on your adventure?

Wow, the first Olympic Games! I've been excited about this all year! All those amazing athletes who have been training their whole lives for –

You just missed the whole thing. While you were buying your chips.

SURVIVE IN TIME

It's time to jump into my time machine again. We're heading for Olympia in 396 BCE, about forty years after the Statue of Zeus was built. There was an Olympic Games held in that year (just like today, the games were held every four years) and, as you'll see, this one was particularly interesting.

Only Greek males were allowed to attend the games. That meant no girls, nobody from outside of Greece and no time-travelling children from the future either. According to the ancient writer Pausanias, the penalty for breaking those rules was to be thrown off the peak of a nearby mountain called Mount Typaion. Ouch!

To try to avoid that happening to you, you're going to want to dress like a Greek boy in a simple brown tunic that comes down to your knees. You'll also need a map and an AI translator. You have two missions: find the Statue of Zeus and meet an Olympic champion.

Good luck, and try not to get thrown off any mountains. You're just starting to grow on me.

***

After the usual vomit-inducing rollercoaster ride, you land on a hill just to the north of Olympia, which gives you a view of the whole site. Olympia is not a town but a collection of temples and sports venues. You can see the roofs of dozens of buildings of every shape and size, with crowds of people moving from one to another like ants. There's a babble of excited chatter rising up through the air and, every now and then, wild cheers of delight.

You set off down the hill, drinking in the sights and sounds. Directly below, you can see the Olympic stadium. It's not shaped in an oval like today's stadiums but a rectangle with four sharp corners.

You enter it via a tunnel and find yourself in a huge crowd standing close together on a slope surrounding the track. As many as 45,000 spectators gather to watch the events, and, as the pilot warned you, all of them are men and boys. It's so unfair that girls are not allowed in to watch the games!

WOMEN IN ANCIENT GREECE

In ancient Greece, women didn't have as much freedom as they do now. In most cities, women usually stayed at home, taking care of the house and children. They didn't have many rights and weren't allowed to vote or own land. The exception was in the city of Sparta, where women could buy property, get an education and even train in sports. In all cities, women played important roles in religious activities, such as being priestesses in temples, but, ultimately the men were in charge.

You find yourself a spot and settle down to watch the events on the track. There is a group of competitors lined up behind a row of white stones, like the starting blocks used in modern races. At first you're completely swept up in the atmosphere and the cheering crowd, and don't notice anything unusual about the runners. But then you see it. You rub your eyes and squint to make sure you're really seeing what you think you are seeing.

All the runners are naked. Completely naked.

Gosh, you think, *the women of ancient Greece might not have had much freedom, but the men sure did. Maybe too much freedom!*

If you want the chance to meet an Olympic champion, you're going to have to stick around to see who wins the race. But that does mean watching eight ancient Greek bottoms running off into the distance. Should you hang around for that, or would you rather explore Olympia to look for the Statue of Zeus?

OPTION 1:
WATCH SOME EVENTS IN
THE OLYMPIC STADIUM
(PAGE 79)

OPTION 2:
EXPLORE THE SITE
OF OLYMPIA
(PAGE 76)

YOU DECIDE TO EXPLORE THE SITE OF OLYMPIA.

You've plenty of time to watch some Olympic events later –
after all, the ancient games went on for five days. You head
to the right of the stadium where there's a long, covered
walkway.

Your map calls it the Echo Stoa and it was built to
separate the stadium from the Temple of Zeus so the god
wouldn't be offended by all the shouting coming from the
excited spectators. It's not a quiet place, however. There are
stalls on both sides selling all kinds of goods, including
pottery, figurines, bags and snacks. Once again, the pilot
failed to provide you with any money, and you now know
better than to help yourself to the food at market stalls.

You come to a building that your map informs you
contains the sanctuary of Hestia, the Greek goddess of the
home. There's a cauldron burning on an altar, the yellow
flame flickering brightly in the shady space. In the modern
Olympic Games, a flame (called the Olympic Flame) is kept
burning throughout the competition, and the flame of Hestia
is where that tradition began.

You check your map again and realize you're not far from the Temple of Zeus, where the statue is located. You make your way in that direction and find a beautiful white structure with a long roof supported by a row of thick columns. There are intricate carvings on the façade at each end of the roof, including one of Pelops and his famous chariot race. When you approach to take a closer look, you see white-robed priests preparing for some kind of ceremony. It might be risky to sneak past them, but on the other hand, this could be your only chance to find the Statue of Zeus. What do you want to do?

OPTION 1:
WATCH SOME EVENTS IN
THE OLYMPIC STADIUM
(PAGE 79)

OPTION 2:
TRY AND SNEAK PAST
THE PRIESTS
(PAGE 86)

STOP FIGHTING!

The Olympic Games were a big deal in ancient Greece, and thousands of people would travel to watch them. The problem was that Greece was not one single country but a collection of independent cities, who were often fighting one another. When there were wars going on, it was too dangerous to travel. So to make sure people could get to Olympia safely for the games, the Greek cities made an agreement not to fight each other for a whole month. One month without war every four years! It doesn't say much for how peaceful they were the rest of the time, does it?

YOU DECIDE TO WATCH SOME EVENTS IN THE OLYMPIC STADIUM.

The sprint race is about to begin. As a judge shouts out, the athletes dash straight down the track, which is nearly 200 metres long. The crowd starts cheering for their favourite runners. In the ancient Olympics, all the competitors are Greek, so the people are cheering for runners from their own city, such as Athens, Sparta or Thebes. In an instant, the race is over and the men around you start jumping up and down with joy. The winner raises his arms in triumph, saluting the crowd.

A judge steps forward and plants a crown of green olive leaves on his head, the ancient equivalent of a gold medal. You wish they'd put the leaves a bit lower down, to be honest, but oh well. What a thrill, watching live races in the birthplace of the Olympic Games! Far more exciting than watching your parents race around a supermarket, like you'd probably be doing if you were back home. You decide to stay to watch more events.

In the next running race, the competitors have to run the length of the track and then back again for a total of almost 400 metres. You also watch a throwing event you recognize from the modern Olympics, the discus. The competitors spin round in a circle and fling a metal disc as far as they can.

After that, there are some fighting events. You watch a

pair of men box each other in a rectangular sand pit in the centre of the stadium. They don't wear gloves like modern boxers but have their hands strapped with leather. You hear a sharp crack when one hits the other, and a disturbing amount of blood pours from his face.

The next fight is even worse. It's called the *pankration* and it's like a mixture of wrestling and boxing. As far as you can tell, there aren't many rules. The two men just attack one another with fists, elbows, knees and feet, either striking or trying to grab hold of each other. It only ends when one of the fighters holds up his hand to admit defeat.

The events were interesting, but you feel you've seen enough naked wrestling athletes for now. Many of the spectators begin to file out of the stadium and head towards the hippodrome, a long track used for chariot racing. But you also notice the *pankration* champion leave in a different direction with a group of his supporters. What should you do?

OPTION 1:
GO TO THE HIPPODROME
(PAGE 84)

OPTION 2:
FOLLOW THE *PANKRATION*
CHAMPION (PAGE 82)

ANCIENT CHAMPIONS

Olympic winners became heroes in their home cities. Some famous ancient champions included Leonidas of Rhodes, who won twelve running races over four consecutive Olympics; Arrichion of Phigalia, who won the *pankration* three times in a row before tragically dying in the last fight; and the six-time wrestling champion Milo of Croton. Known for his massive appetite, Milo brought a cow to Olympia as a sacrifice to Zeus and then ate it all himself in one day.

Buuuurp. Any chance of seconds?

YOU DECIDE TO FOLLOW THE *PANKRATION* CHAMPION.

The man and his supporters stride through Olympia, voices raised in triumph. They head for a large rectangular courtyard in the far north-west corner, where there's a hive of sporting activity. There are competitors lifting heavy stones to warm up their muscles, practising wrestling moves with one another, or hurling shot puts and javelins. You look at your map and realize you're in the gymnasium, a word we still use today.

Suddenly the champion spins around and claps you on the shoulder. 'Hello, boy. I noticed you following me! You're interested in the *pankration*, eh? Come on! I'll teach you!'

You panic. The man is enormous, like a giant statue made of chiselled stone. You suspect he could break every bone in your body simply by looking at you fiercely.

'Don't be shy, boy! I won't hurt you! Get into your fighting stance!'

Hesitantly you strike up what you imagine is a wrestling pose. The champion throws his head back and lets out a roar of laughter. 'What are you doing, boy?'

Before you can think of an excuse not to fight the giant standing before you, he grabs you by the neck of your tunic and lifts you off the ground. There's a clatter as the AI translation device falls to the ground.

'Wait a minute, what's that? I've never seen anything like it before. You can't be Greek!'

He starts to drag you out of the gymnasium, his friends following angrily.

'Hey, where are you taking me?' you cry.

'The peak of Mount Typaion,' comes the stone-cold reply.

'For a hike?' you ask hopefully.

'No, sunshine. Not for a hike.'

Come on! Just throw me over your shoulder or something!

OPTION 1:
ACTIVATE YOUR SPECIAL WATCH (PAGE 96)

OPTION 2:
PERSUADE THE CHAMPION TO LET YOU GO (PAGE 86)

YOU DECIDE TO GO TO THE HIPPODROME.

Chariot racing was the most popular of all the Olympic sports, and the crowd is buzzing with excitement round the long, oblong track. You fight your way to the front and see that a race is about to start. Six chariots, each with four horses and one driver, are parading round the track. The chariots are decorated in different colours, and the spectators cheer when their own city's representative trundles past. The horses look incredibly powerful, their sleek bodies rippling with muscle. The drivers pull on their reins to keep them steady.

They make their way to the start line, and the crowd falls silent in anticipation. Then they're off! The sound of twenty-four horses pounding forward splits the air like thunder. The chariots move at amazing speed, the two-wheeled carriages coming perilously close to touching as they power down the track. You look at the drivers as they ride past, their faces grim with determination as they flick the reins one way and then another. They reach the end of the course and turn around a pole to head back, the wheels of the chariots skidding through the dirt. How do they not crash? The skill of the horses and drivers is astonishing!

A lap is completed, then two, three, four. Two of the chariots pull ahead, vying for the lead. Then, disaster! As they swing round the pole, their wheels collide and one of the drivers is flung out of his carriage! He flies through the air and lands with a bruising thud. You imagine he wishes he was wearing armour, or at least some pants.

His horses veer off the course out of control, but the other five competitors continue without a glance. The race goes on. Three chariots are challenging for the lead now, and the noise of the crowd becomes deafening. Eight laps, nine, ten, eleven. The final lap!

A blue chariot is winning but a red one is gaining fast. You hold your breath, eyes glued to the race. This event should be in the modern Olympics! It's definitely better than synchronized swimming. They approach the finish line and . . . the red chariot wins! The crowd erupts with feverish cheers. What a race!

You're breathless with excitement, but what to do next? You could watch the winning ceremony to see the champion collect their crown, or go to the Temple of Zeus to find the statue.

OPTION 1:
WATCH THE WINNING
CEREMONY (PAGE 87)

OPTION 2:
GO TO THE TEMPLE OF
ZEUS (PAGE 90)

THAT DIDN'T WORK OUT FOR YOU, UNFORTUNATELY.

You get dragged to the top of Mount Typaion and discover the hard way that children can't fly. But there's no need to be upset! The following letter will be provided to anyone interested in your whereabouts:

Dear parent, guardian, teacher or interested person,

It is with great regret that we inform you of the loss of [insert name here] in Olympia. It appears they failed to return to the transport vehicle by the scheduled time. Although at this point it is difficult to know where (or when) they are, we can assure you we are doing everything in our power to find them.

Please be aware that [insert name here] was clearly warned of the risks involved with their journey. The company cannot, therefore, take any financial responsibility for their disappearance.

Yours sincerely,

Intrepid Explorers Inc.

Think you could do better next time?
Go back and start again on page 72!

YOU DECIDE TO WATCH THE WINNING CEREMONY.

A judge in a white cloak enters the arena, holding up a crown of olive leaves. The winning driver dismounts from his chariot, and you wait for him to receive the crown. But he walks away, giving a final wave to the crowd. The judge raises his arms and shouts out in a loud, clear voice: 'The winner of the four-horse chariot race is . . . Cynisca of Sparta!'

To your surprise, a woman enters the arena; in fact, it's the first woman you've seen all day. The crowd fall silent, seemingly as astonished as you are. But when the judge lays the wreath on her head, they start to clap and cheer. Cynisca owns the chariot and horses that won the race, and so *she* is the Olympic Champion. But she's not just any Olympic Champion – she's the first-ever female winner at the Olympic Games!

Is this the reason the pilot chose to land in this particular year? As the crowd starts to disperse, you stay where you are, looking for a chance to talk to Cynisca. You notice her leave the hippodrome and hurry to catch up with her.

'Excuse me, er . . .' You realize you don't know the proper way to address a Spartan princess. '. . . Your Royal Spartanness. Congratulations!'

She turns and smiles. 'Thank you. Did you enjoy the race?'

'Yes, it was amazing!' you reply. 'So much better than synchronized swimming.'

'*What swimming?*' Cynisca looks confused. 'Come, walk with me. I'm going to give thanks for my victory.'

Wow. You've met an Olympic champion – the first female one! – and completed one part of your mission. Could Cynisca help you find the Statue of Zeus and complete the next part, or will you use your map to find the temple yourself?

I'd like to see *you* try this.

OPTION I:
GO TO THE TEMPLE OF ZEUS (PAGE 90)

OPTION 2:
WALK WITH CYNISCA (PAGE 92)

SPARTA

The two most powerful cities in ancient Greece were Athens and Sparta. They were rivals and had very different cultures. Athens was famous for its philosophers, playwrights and politicians. They loved to talk, learn and be creative. Sparta, however, had a much harsher way of life. For instance, boys didn't grow up living with their parents. At the age of seven, they moved into a military barracks and trained to become soldiers – whether they wanted to or not. They were given one item of clothing per year and had to find most of their own food. (This didn't mean sneaking into the biscuit tin while no one was looking, but hunting and trapping animals.) Girls didn't become soldiers, but they practised wrestling, boxing and horse riding. They were like a nation of action heroes.

YOU DECIDE TO GO TO THE TEMPLE OF ZEUS.

You locate the temple on the map and head on your way. Near your destination, you discover a large crowd has assembled. Unlike the noisy, cheering spectators at the sports events, everyone here is quiet and respectful, watching as priests emerge from the temple wearing long white robes. The priests take their place behind a stone altar and begin a melodious chant. Incense burns all around, filling the air with a sweet and mysterious scent. The men in the crowd begin to pray, raising their arms to the heavens and calling for Zeus to bless them. Suddenly a figure steps forward with an ox and leads it towards the altar. You notice one of the priests is carrying a large knife. He's going to sacrifice the ox as an offering to Zeus.

You'd rather avoid witnessing an animal sacrifice, so you leave the ceremony and walk over to the temple, searching for a way to get inside. The Statue of Zeus must be in there somewhere! The temple has thirteen beautiful white columns on each side and six columns at each end. You peer between them to try to catch a glimpse of the great statue, but when you step closer, an angry voice calls out.

'Clear off, boy! Go back to your father!'

A priest is glaring at you fiercely and, remembering the penalty for breaking the rules in Olympia, you hastily retreat. When you return to the ceremony, you're relieved to find the sacrifice is over. The meat from the ox is now sizzling over a large fire ready to be eaten. You wonder if Milo of Croton will turn up and eat it all in one go.

Suddenly your special watch starts to flash. It's a message from the pilot telling you it's time to go. But you still haven't seen the Statue of Zeus!

OPTION 1:
TRY AND SNEAK INTO
THE TEMPLE (PAGE 86)

OPTION 2:
ACTIVATE YOUR SPECIAL
WATCH (PAGE 96)

YOU DECIDE TO WALK WITH CYNISCA.

She tells you all about her life in Sparta. She's the sister of the king, Agesilaus II, a very powerful and ambitious ruler. It was her brother's idea that she train horses in order to take part in the Olympics.

'He thought I could win glory for Sparta, and today I did!' she says proudly.

You congratulate her. 'In the future, lots of women will compete in the Olympics. In all the events, just like men.'

The princess eyes you strangely. 'In the future? How could you . . .?' She pauses. 'Well, I hope so. In Sparta, girls are encouraged to do sports. But in the rest of Greece, not so much.'

She falls silent as she reaches her destination. You look up and find yourself in front of a giant statue of a bearded man seated on a great throne. The Statue of Zeus! It's over twelve metres high, so tall it barely fits under the temple roof. The base of the statue is made of black marble, and Zeus himself is ivory and gold: ivory for his skin and gold for his beard, robes and staff. The ivory makes his skin look real, and the gold gives him power and strength. It looks incredibly lifelike and you can understand why the Greeks travel from all over to see it. On the base of the statue are pictures showing the tales of Greek mythology along with an inscription. 'Phidias, son of Charmides, an Athenian, made me,' reads Cynisca. 'He was a genius . . . for an Athenian.'

Hmm . . . perhaps *too* lifelike?

You glance at her. 'You don't like Athenians?'

Cynisca laughs. 'Of course not – I'm a Spartan! We're deadly rivals! You're a funny one. You know the future but not the present!' She gives you a shrewd look. 'Well, interesting little child, I have to return to my horses. Have a safe trip back to . . . wherever you're from.'

You thank her and say goodbye, watching her long white dress swish at her ankles as she walks swiftly away. Your mission is completed, but just as you turn to head off back to the time machine, you notice a group of supporters surrounding a powerful-looking athlete. You recognize him immediately – it's the *pankration* champion you watched in the stadium! Is there time for one last adventure to see where he's going?

OPTION 1:
FOLLOW THE *PANKRATION*
CHAMPION (PAGE 82)

OPTION 2:
WALK BACK TO THE TIME
MACHINE (PAGE 95)

FROM ANCIENT TO MODERN

The ancient Olympic Games were banned by a Roman emperor named Theodosius in 393 CE. He was a Christian and didn't want people worshipping the old Greek gods. He's said to have taken the Statue of Zeus, which was over 800 years old, to his home in Constantinople in Turkey, where it was lost in a fire a few decades later. Olympia was forgotten about for centuries, and its temples and stadium fell into ruin. But eventually archaeologists excavated the site and discovered the remains of the ancient buildings.

When Athens hosted the modern Olympic Games in 2004, they held the shot-put event in the original stadium of Olympia. It was a truly historic moment, as competitors walked past the remains of the temples of Zeus and Hera on the way to their event, just like the Greek athletes did thousands of years ago. Except they had clothes on.

CONGRATULATIONS! YOU COMPLETED YOUR MISSION!

You met an Olympic champion, Cynisca of Sparta, and saw the Statue of Zeus. The pilot smiles as you approach the time machine.

'How were the Olympics?'

'Great!' you reply. 'The athletes were amazing!'

'Wonderful news, and, in even better news, I'm pretty sure people will keep their clothes on at our next destination. We're going to the Mausoleum of Halicarnassus.'

'The Mauso–?'

'Don't worry, I'll explain on the way.'

YOU ACTIVATE YOUR SPECIAL WATCH AND RETURN TO THE TIME MACHINE.

The pilot greets you as you appear.

'Oh, you're back! You didn't get thrown off a mountain then,' he says brightly. 'Now that's a real surprise.'

'Right . . .' you reply. Sometimes you wonder whether time-travelling was actually a good idea. 'Where are we going next?'

'The Mausoleum of Halicarnassus.'

'The what?'

'Don't worry, you'll understand soon enough.'

Feeling brave enough to give it another try?

Go back to page 72!

CHAPTER 4:
THE MAUSOLEUM OF HALICARNASSUS

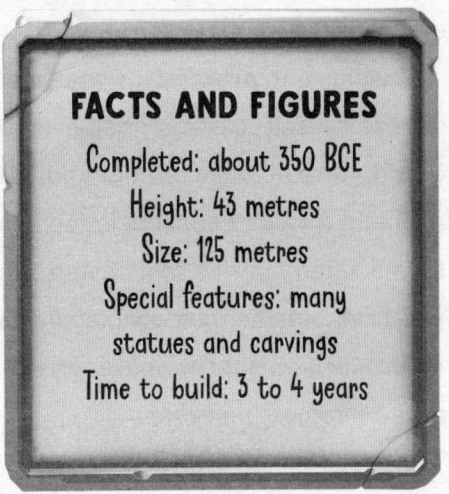

FACTS AND FIGURES

Completed: about 350 BCE
Height: 43 metres
Size: 125 metres
Special features: many
statues and carvings
Time to build: 3 to 4 years

WELCOME TO HALICARNASSUS!

A mausoleum is a fancy word for a tomb. The word comes
from King Mausolus, who ruled a small kingdom called
Caria in Asia Minor (modern-day Turkey) from 377 to
353 BCE. When he died, his beloved wife, Artemisia II,
built a magnificent tomb for him in their capital city of
Halicarnassus.

Caria was under the control of the Persian Empire,
one of the most powerful empires in history. But when

Mausolus and his sister-wife, Artemisia II, came to the throne, the two rulers decided to make their kingdom stronger than it had ever been. So they –

Wooah, hold on a second! Did you just say sister-wife? As in, a sister who was also his wife?

Ah, yes, Mausolus and Artemisia, whose love for each other was so great it inspired one of the Seven Wonders of the Ancient World, were actually brother and sister, which is entirely gross. But it wasn't unusual in the ancient world. Egyptian pharaohs often married their sisters, as they believed no one from outside their own family had the right to rule. It probably also meant they never grew out of fighting over the TV remote control.

HAIR TODAY, GONE TOMORROW

The king and queen decided to make their kingdom more powerful by moving their capital city from Mylasa to Halicarnassus, a port on the Aegean Sea. Halicarnassus was just a small town at the time, but the royal couple were determined to make it one of the most beautiful cities in the world. They built temples, theatres and monuments, forcing people to pay high taxes to cover the expense. There's even a story they taxed people's hair! Apparently long hair was fashionable for men in Caria, but Mausolus told his subjects he'd been ordered to send hair to Persia to make wigs. The men didn't want to cut their hair because they enjoyed looking like models in a shampoo commercial, so Mausolus gave them a choice of either cutting their hair or paying a tax to keep it long.

SHHH, DON'T TELL ANYONE

Thanks to the hair-raisingly high taxes, Halicarnassus soon became home to many beautiful buildings made of marble and stone. But why did Mausolus want to build a capital there in the first place? The answer is that Halicarnassus had two natural harbours: one that was easily visible from the sea and another that was hidden by a spit of land.

Caria had always been famous for its seafaring and shipbuilding, and Mausolus wanted a place to keep his kingdom's navy. His plan was to use this secret harbour to hide his warships. As we'll see during our next trip, this secret harbour was going to prove very useful.

BIG TOMB FOR A BIG HEAD

Mausolus was a very proud man who believed he deserved all the best things in life – and death. He decided to build a tomb for himself that everyone would admire and envy. Unfortunately he died in 353 BCE before it could be finished. Luckily his wife Artemisia was determined to complete his vision. She employed the greatest sculptors of the age, tasking them with creating the most beautiful building the world had ever known.

SURVIVE IN TIME

You've probably learned by now that travel is at your own risk and there's no guarantee you'll return safely. Keep that in mind as we set off for 352 BCE, a year after the death of King Mausolus. What's so dangerous about 352 BCE, I hear you ask? Well, after Mausolus died, the nearby Greek island of Rhodes decided to invade Halicarnassus. They thought Queen Artemisia wouldn't be able to defend the kingdom by herself just because she was a woman.

Want to see if they were right? Hop into the time machine and let's find out. Your mission this time is very simple: explore the Mausoleum of Halicarnassus. Even you can't mess that up, surely? Although the mausoleum wasn't quite finished in 352 BCE, you should still get a good idea of how impressive it was.

Here's your AI translator and your usual brown tunic. You won't need a map this time as the mausoleum will be easy to find. Good luck, and don't get caught up in anything you can't get out of!

***

You land on a hill overlooking Halicarnassus. Stepping out of the time machine, you see the whole city spread out below you, an expanse of closely packed houses with reddish roofs. Fishing boats bob about in the harbour, while tiny workers are busy on the quays, loading and unloading goods.

In the centre of the city is a cluster of marble palaces and temples decorated with rows of white columns. Right in the middle of them is a taller structure, gleaming in the sunshine. It looks beautiful but doesn't seem finished. You can see men hard at work on it. Could it be the Mausoleum of Halicarnassus?

You hurry down the hill and make straight for the tall building, passing through a gate in the city walls. It's easy to find the way, as there's a main street leading right to the centre that is wider than the alleys threading between the houses. The pilot was right. This is going to be the easiest mission ever!

It doesn't take long to reach your destination.

'Hey you, child! Come here a second!' A man is calling to you from an alley, eagerly waving his hand in a friendly gesture.

OPTION 1:
APPROACH THE
STRANGER (PAGE 104)

OPTION 2:
TRY TO ENTER THE
MAUSOLEUM (PAGE 106)

ANCIENT WARSHIPS

What kind of ships were hiding in Halicarnassus's secret harbour? They were most likely triremes: fast, sleek vessels with three rows of oars on each side, powered by strong rowers. At the front they had a bronze-covered ram to crash into enemy ships. They also had sails to catch the wind and move faster.

YOU DECIDE TO APPROACH THE STRANGER.

I mean, it's not like you were ever warned not to talk to strangers, right? What's the worst that could happen? Apart from getting thrown into a dungeon, sold into slavery or flung off the city walls, that is.

The man is wearing a Greek-style tunic and has a trimmed beard and short hair. Obviously a Carian citizen who isn't scared of scissors.

'How would you like to earn some money, child?' he whispers.

You hesitate. 'Er . . . I'm just here to see the Mausoleum of Halicarnassus.'

'Oh, the king's tomb?' He draws you in and puts his arm round your shoulder. 'You'll never get past all the workers. They're very protective of the tomb. But I could get you in if you do me a little favour first: I need you to go down to the harbour and tell me what you see and hear. Especially from any soldiers that are around.'

Snoop around the harbour and spy on soldiers? That sounds quite high on the list of things that could get you thrown into a dungeon. But also a pretty awesome adventure.

'So, do we have a deal? As soon as you come back, I'll get you into the tomb.'

This is a tough decision to make . . .

OPTION 1:
TRY TO ENTER THE
MAUSOLEUM (PAGE 106)

OPTION 2:
AGREE TO HELP THE
STRANGER (PAGE 109)

YOU TRY TO ENTER THE MAUSOLEUM.

There are hundreds of men occupied around the marble structure. Some are labourers hauling on thick ropes to lift heavy slabs of stone up into the air. Others are craftsmen working on blocks of marble, smoothing and polishing the sides until they shine. One man seems to be an artist. He's carving a picture into one of the polished blocks. You lean in closer and see a vibrant scene of a chariot race, just like the one you watched in Olympia. Two chariots are racing side by side, each set of horses straining their muscular bodies to get ahead. It looks incredibly real, and you marvel at the skill of the artist as he chips away one tiny piece of marble at a time. One slip and he'll have to start all over again.

'Oi! What do you think you're doing here?' a muscled workman bellows out from behind you.

You swing round in fright and feel your elbow hit something. The artist let outs a howl of anguish.

'You fool! You've ruined it!'

You realize your elbow knocked the man's chisel, and now one of the horses has a hole in its leg. It's certainly not going to win the chariot race like that.

'Take this urchin away and drown it in the sea!' the artist cries.

A group of workers comes towards you with arms outstretched and, without a second's thought, you flee.

You dash away from the construction site with the furious men close behind.

Suddenly a hand grabs you from nowhere and pulls you through a doorway. As your eyes adjust to the dark, you realize who your unlikely hero is. It's the stranger from the alley! He hisses into your ear as the workers head off in different directions to find you.

'I need you to go to the harbour and tell me what you see and hear the soldiers talking about. I'll take care of the workmen and get you into the mausoleum if you promise to help. Meet me back here when you're done.'

You aren't sure who you should be more worried about – the spying stranger hiding in alleyways or the angry men whose handiwork you just ruined.

OPTION 1:
FACE THE WORKERS AND APOLOGIZE TO THE ARTIST (PAGE 111)

OPTION 2:
AGREE TO HELP THE STRANGER (PAGE 109)

WHO'S THE BEST ARTIST?

The Mausoleum of Halicarnassus took three or four years to build. Sadly, Queen Artemisia died before it was completed, but the workers continued to labour on it. This is because the artists were competing with each other to see who could create the most magnificent statues and carvings. Each artist took charge of one of the four sides of the tomb, and they decided to keep going until their work was complete.

YOU AGREE TO HELP THE STRANGER.

He points you in the direction of the harbour and you set off at a fast walk, anxious to get your mission over and done with. As you get closer, you see people rushing through the narrow streets looking fearful and panicked. Some are heading towards the harbour and others away from it. What's going on?

You hurry on and find yourself in a large crowd of men and women, all staring out across the sea and pointing. You weave your way to the front and follow their gaze. Far out on the horizon, you can make out a long line of white sails approaching. The fishing boats you'd seen from the hill are hurrying back into port, unloading their catches as fast as they can. There's a feeling of dread in the air. Those white sails can't be good news.

Suddenly the crowd parts. A group of soldiers march through the gap towards the port followed by a black-haired woman. She's wearing a flowing blue dress with a gold chain around her neck and jewelled bracelets on her arms. When the soldiers point towards the sails, she nods thoughtfully and whispers an instruction to the soldier at the front. He bows to her and hurries away.

The woman remains on the harbour, looking out at the sea. You notice a sadness in her eyes; a loneliness that seems to make her unaware of the hurried fishermen rushing around her.

This must be Queen Artemisia, and she is probably thinking about her husband, King Mausolus, who died less than a year ago.

It looks like things are about to get interesting, or very, very dangerous. Do you want to stick around?

OPTION 1:
SEE WHAT QUEEN ARTEMISIA DOES
(PAGE 115)

OPTION 2:
EXPLORE THE SURROUNDING AREA
(PAGE 112)

WRONG CHOICE.

You find yourself picked up, dragged on to a boat and flung into the deep blue sea. But not to worry! The following letter will be provided to anyone interested in your whereabouts:

Dear parent, guardian, teacher or interested person,

It is with great regret that we inform you of the loss of [insert name here] in Halicarnassus. It appears they failed to return to the transport vehicle by the scheduled time. Although at this point it is difficult to know where (or when) they are, we can assure you we are doing everything in our power to find them.

Please be aware that [insert name here] was clearly warned of the risks involved with their journey. The company cannot, therefore, take any financial responsibility for their disappearance.

Yours sincerely,

Intrepid Explorers Inc.

Think you could do better next time?
Go back and start again on page 101!

YOU DECIDE TO EXPLORE THE SURROUNDING AREA.

You don't feel confident about getting into the mausoleum and you don't want to bump into the stranger again. The streets away from the harbour are quiet, as if everyone has rushed home to prepare for whatever is coming. You wander along until you find yourself in a large outdoor arena. It's in the shape of a semi-circle, with a stage at one end and a rising bank of stone seats around the sides. You guess as many as 10,000 people could fit inside. There's no one in the seats now, but on the stage you can see a group of actors rehearsing for a play.

'That's *Medea*,' a familiar voice murmurs behind you. 'A play by Euripides.'

You swing round to see the stranger from the alley. Has he followed you here? 'Eu-rip-i-dees? Who?'

'Euripides pants and you'll buy me a new pair. Ha ha ha!' he replies. He looks disappointed at your look of total confusion. 'Never mind. What did you find out from the harbour?'

You tell him you saw ships on the horizon and a lady you guessed was the queen.

'So, the Rhodes invasion has begun,' the stranger says, stroking his beard thoughtfully. 'I need you to go back and see what Queen Artemisia does next.'

That sounds dangerous. 'What if I don't want to?'

The man shrugs his shoulders and gives you a grave look.

'Well, it's dangerous for a child like you to be wandering around during an invasion. I'd hate for something terrible to happen to you.' Then his expression brightens. 'But if you help me, I'm sure I can protect you. I'll get you into the king's tomb and this will all end happily.'

You're really starting to question whether this man is to be trusted, but you also dread to think what might happen if you say no. Do you want to head back to the harbour and see what the queen does next? Or stand your ground and tell the strange man to do his own dirty work!

OPTION 1:
SEE WHAT QUEEN
ARTEMISIA DOES
(PAGE 115)

OPTION 2:
REFUSE TO HELP
(PAGE 111)

WHAT A TRAGEDY!

Euripides was a famous Greek playwright. He wrote tragedies – sad stories that usually ended in a disaster, a bit like when England play football. Other writers, like Aristophanes, wrote comedies that poked fun at Greek society and politics. The plays were very sophisticated. They used special effects for dramatic scenes, like smoke and fire, and drums to simulate thunder. They even had machinery to lower characters on to the stage.

When I shout action, miss the penalty!

YOU DECIDE TO SEE WHAT QUEEN ARTEMISIA DOES.

She stays on the harbour for a while as the white sails slowly get closer. But eventually she heads off with her soldiers. The group hurries along the edge of the bay and you follow nervously, keeping your distance so you don't get spotted. All of a sudden, the soldiers disappear from view. Where did they go?

Taking a deep breath to calm yourself, you creep forward in the same direction. You reach the point where they vanished and, all of a sudden, a whole fleet of warships comes into view, floating in the calm blue water. The navy of the kingdom of Caria.

You're in the secret harbour of Halicarnassus! This is the reason King Mausolus decided to build his capital here in the first place. Separated from the main harbour, it's concealed by a long spit of land that curves out into the sea, blocking it from the view of approaching ships.

You catch sight of Queen Artemisia as she orders her soldiers on to the ships. There are hundreds of them, serious men with metal swords swinging at their sides. The invaders from Rhodes will have no idea that they're here! The queen turns to one of her commanders, and you strain your ears to catch what she's saying.

'Listen for the shouts in the market square and then attack.'

The commander salutes and hurries off to join his men. Queen Artemisia heads back towards the main harbour, flanked by her guards. You have new information for the stranger now. Should you tell him what's going on so he can get you into the mausoleum before the invaders arrive, or are there more secrets to uncover?

OPTION 1:
REPORT TO THE STRANGER (PAGE 117)

OPTION 2:
KEEP FOLLOWING THE QUEEN (PAGE 119)

YOU DECIDE TO REPORT TO THE STRANGER.

He is waiting in the alley where you first met him. He beckons you over with a furtive wave and leads you into the shadows.

'What's happening?' he asks, his tone urgent and serious.

You don't answer, suddenly nervous. Should you really be here?

'Tell me now and I'll get you into the tomb. I've bribed the workers to let you enter.'

Exploring the mausoleum is your mission. Perhaps this is the only way to succeed. You take a deep breath and start to talk.

'There he is! Get him!'

You're interrupted by an angry shout. Before you can move, a troop of soldiers are rushing at you, swords drawn. You wonder what you've done this time, but they push you out the way and grab the stranger with rough hands.

'Caught you at last, spy!' the leader of the guards growls. 'Thought you could sabotage our queen's plans? Caria will never fall to Rhodes!'

The spy struggles helplessly, his face frantic. 'No woman can rule a kingdom! Rhodes must be victorious!'

The soldiers ignore his protests and drag him away. One of them points at you with his sword. 'What shall we do with the child?'

The commander shrugs. 'Drown the pint-sized traitor in the sea.'

OPTION 1:
ACTIVATE YOUR SPECIAL WATCH (PAGE 126)

OPTION 2:
TRY TO NEGOTIATE FOR YOUR FREEDOM
(PAGE 111)

BADASS QUEENS

The spy was, of course, wrong about women being unable to rule a kingdom. Caria previously had another Queen Artemisia, who commanded her own fleet at a famous naval battle in 480 BCE. She was so good at it that the Persian emperor came to her for advice on military tactics. Egypt also had a brilliant female ruler: Pharaoh Hatshepsut. She reigned for more than twenty years from 1479 BCE, bringing peace, strength and prosperity to her people. Then there was Queen Zenobia of Syria, who took on the might of the Roman Empire. She could shoot arrows with perfect aim while riding on a horse and, according to Roman historians, had teeth so dazzlingly white people thought they were pearls.

YOU DECIDE TO KEEP FOLLOWING THE QUEEN.

Artemisia returns to the harbour where the ships from Rhodes have got much closer. You can see the faces of the sailors now as they pull on the oars of the leading vessel, while on the deck scowling soldiers have bows and arrows raised for firing.

The queen steps to the edge of the harbour, apparently unconcerned. Calmly she opens her arms as though welcoming the invaders to shoot. At the same time, her guards hold up their swords and slowly lay them on the ground. They're surrendering!

The ships reach the harbour, and the Rhodes soldiers jump down on to the beach, their boots splashing through the shallow water. They're led by a large man wearing a magnificent helmet with a tall crest of red feathers. The queen joins the invaders at the water's edge and says something to the red-crested commander. He follows her through a large wooden gate into a spacious market square with half of his men marching on behind. The commander takes off his helmet and speaks in a loud voice: 'My name is General Mentor. I accept your surrender to Rhodes.'

Queen Artemisia smiles. 'We welcome you to our city, General Mentor. Please accept some refreshments after your long journey.'

She claps her hands, and a flurry of servants bring jugs of wine and water. Upon a nod from their commander, the soldiers from Rhodes take off their helmets and drink thirstily. But they wouldn't be drinking so calmly if they could see what you can see from the edge of the square.

Hidden on the roofs of the surrounding houses are hundreds of Carian soldiers. They have their eyes on Queen Artemisia, who abruptly steps back and retreats into the shadows. There is a loud shout before arrows begin raining down on the invaders from all sides. In a panic, the men from Rhodes rush towards the gate, only to find it already closed. They're trapped!

From the harbour comes the sounds of battle, as Artemisia's hidden navy falls on Mentor's undefended fleet. The general throws down his sword and surrenders.

Now you really have some news to share with the stranger. He's definitely creepy, but he might be your only chance of getting into the mausoleum. Unless you sneak away and find it yourself . . .

OPTION 1:
REPORT TO THE
STRANGER (PAGE 117)

OPTION 2:
SNEAK AWAY FROM THE
MARKET SQUARE
(PAGE 122)

SNEAKY TACTICS

The trick Artemisia played on the invaders from Rhodes wasn't the only time sneaky tactics were used in ancient battles. Remember the city of Babylon we visited in Chapter 2? When Cyrus the Great of Persia attacked it in 539 BCE, he couldn't break through the high city walls. So instead, he dug through the banks of the Euphrates to redirect the water into another course. The point where the river entered Babylon was left as a dry bed, allowing his soldiers to march along it and under the walls of the city.

BABYLONIAN 1:
Shouldn't we fight back?

BABYLONIAN 2:
We were only told to stop them getting *over* the walls.

YOU DECIDE TO SNEAK AWAY FROM THE MARKET SQUARE.
You can hear the people of Halicarnassus celebrating together as the soldiers of Rhodes are taken prisoner. Now might finally be your chance to get a proper look at King Mausolus's tomb. You make your way up to the mausoleum, where you're relieved to find the artists and workers have disappeared and the site is deserted.

Even though it's not finished, you can see it's an amazing structure. It stands the best part of forty-five metres in height – about as tall as the Statue of Liberty from torch to foot – and it's in the shape of a square. But it's the artwork that's truly impressive. At the bottom is a marble base with scenes from Greek mythology carved into the stone. One scene shows strange creatures called centaurs that are half-man and half-horse, while others depict battles between powerful Greek warriors. Above the base are white columns with statues between them. There are Greek gods and goddesses, muscled warriors, and in the centre is a bearded man and a beautiful woman standing side by side: King Mausolus and Queen Artemisia.

On top of the columns is a roof in the shape of a pyramid, with stone steps leading to the top. At the base of the pyramid are yet more statues, this time of powerful, prowling lions. At the very top is a platform where the largest and most magnificent sculpture of all is being carved: a chariot pulled by four horses.

You explore the mausoleum until your watch begins to flash. It's a message from the pilot telling you it's time to go. As you stroll back towards the time machine on the hill, you notice a disturbance in one of the alleys. A man is being arrested by a group of soldiers. You catch a glimpse of his face before the guards drag him away: the stranger who wanted your help.

With short hair like that, he had to be up to no good.

OPTION 1:
RETURN TO THE TIME MACHINE (PAGE 125)

OPTION 2:
TRY TO HELP THE STRANGER (PAGE 111)

A REAL GREEK SPY

There were lots of spies in ancient Greece, including Ephialtes, who betrayed his home of Sparta by helping the Persian Empire. In 480 BCE, the Persians invaded Greece through a narrow mountain pass called Thermopylae. They had more than 250,000 soldiers and were faced by a Greek force of just 10,000. But the Greeks were led by Spartans, who, as we learned in the last chapter, trained to fight from the age of seven. Fighting a battle they couldn't possibly win was their idea of fun. The Persians shot so many arrows in the air they blocked out the Sun, and the Spartan king remarked: 'Isn't it nice to fight in the shade?' He was too cool for words.

For two days, the Spartans held the enemy off. But then Ephialtes did his dirty deed. He told the Persians of a secret path through the mountains that would allow them to attack the Greeks from the rear. Even the Spartans couldn't stop that. The king and his soldiers died defending their land.

CONGRATULATIONS! YOU COMPLETED YOUR MISSION!

You explored the Mausoleum of Halicarnassus and resisted the temptation to betray Queen Artemisia and share her plan with a spy.

The pilot pops his head out of the time machine.

'You didn't drown then,' he says by way of greeting.

Is it your imagination or does he sound disappointed?

'Not this time,' you reply. 'Where are we going next?'

'The Colossus of Rhodes.'

'Rhodes? The island that just attacked Halicarnassus?'

'Yes, but don't worry, it'll be a hundred years later so they should have forgotten you didn't help their spy. Hopefully, anyway!'

YOU ACTIVATE YOUR SPECIAL WATCH AND RETURN TO THE TIME MACHINE.

Unfortunately you didn't manage to complete your mission. The pilot gives you a look of exasperation.

'Couldn't you tell that man was a spy? Why did you go back to him?'

You kick your sandals through the dirt and don't respond.

'You do realize we're time-travelling, don't you? If that spy had foiled Queen Artemisia's plan, it could have changed the entire course of history!'

'Well, he didn't, did he?'

'No, I suppose not.' The pilot shrugs. 'Now strap in. We'll be heading to the spy's homeland for our next strip – Rhodes! But it will be a hundred years later, so I don't think you'll be seeing him again. Even if the Carian soldiers didn't dump him in the sea, he'd be pretty old.'

As the time machine takes off, you pray you'll have better luck next time.

Feeling brave enough to give it another try?
Go back to page 101!

126 THE MAUSOLEUM AT HALICARNASSUS

CHAPTER 5:
THE COLOSSUS OF RHODES

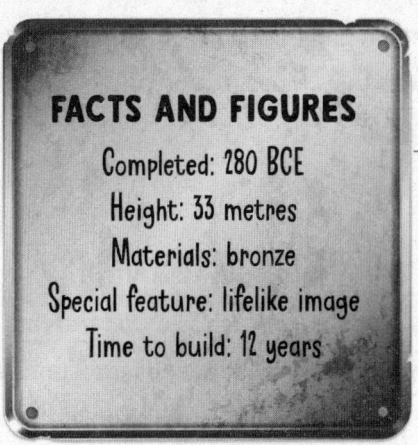

FACTS AND FIGURES

Completed: 280 BCE

Height: 33 metres

Materials: bronze

Special feature: lifelike image

Time to build: 12 years

WELCOME TO RHODES!

Rhodes might have seemed like the bad guy in the last chapter, but the truth was that wars between kingdoms in the ancient world happened all the time, and it's hard to judge today who was right and wrong. (It's like a squabble between two classmates and the teacher doesn't know who started it. The main difference being the helmets and really sharp swords.)

In fact, Rhodes was one of the great cities of Greece. Located on an island of the same name in the eastern

Mediterranean Sea, it was a wealthy centre of trade, culture and learning, famous for its ships, its schools and its grand architecture. It had high city walls to protect it from attacks, two main harbours from which its ships sailed and streets filled with temples, fountains and statues. The most famous statue of all was the Colossus, one of the Seven Wonders of the Ancient World.

GREEKS VERSUS GOATS?

How did the Colossus get built? To understand, we need to start with one of the most successful conquerors of ancient times, Alexander the Great. Alexander was the son of King Philip II, the ruler of Macedon, a kingdom just north of Greece. The Greeks had always looked down on their northern neighbours, viewing Macedon as a poor and backwards place. 'We write poetry and plays, discuss politics and philosophy, and vote in elections,' the Greeks said. 'You Macedonians just herd goats!'

Philip II and his son Alexander, however, were determined to change this attitude. They built up a large and well-trained army (of people, not goats) and marched south into Greece.

Rhodes was an independent kingdom and, as it was not on the Greek mainland, it was presented with a choice: to join the Greeks or the Macedonians.

'Hey, Rhodes, come and join our team!' said the Greeks. 'We have philosophy, plays, and Olympians who wrestle in the nude! We'll win easily!'

'No, support our invasion!' responded the Macedonians. 'We'll give you some goats!'

Rhodes calculated that the Macedonians were stronger than the Greeks and decided to support Philip II. This turned out to be the sensible choice, since the Macedonians won. When Philip's son Alexander became king in 336 BCE, Rhodes became one of his allies, supporting his military campaigns while keeping its independence.

We may have to rethink the helmet.

LET THE GOOD TIMES ROLL!

During Alexander's reign, the young king wasn't satisfied with merely taking over Greece. He wanted to create the biggest empire there had ever been. Despite being just twenty years old, he was a brilliant general and managed to defeat every army he fought against, including the mighty Persian Empire. In the end, his lands stretched from Macedonia all the way to northern India.

Unfortunately the great conqueror died from an illness at the young age of thirty-two. With no one to inherit his throne, four of his Macedonian generals divided up the empire between them. One of them, Ptolemy, took over Egypt and made an alliance with Rhodes. Together, Egypt and Rhodes were able to control the trade in the region, with ships from Rhodes buying and selling ceramics, textiles, jewellery, olive oil, wine and many other goods.

It was a peaceful and prosperous time, and Rhodes used its wealth to open schools that taught philosophy, science and public speaking. Many scholars travelled there to teach and learn.

Some were followers of Aristotle, who was the greatest philosopher of his day. Aristotle taught his pupils to think about the world while strolling around open spaces, as he believed that walking stimulated the mind. Try using this as an excuse next time your teacher tells you to stay in your seat at school.

THE COLOSSUS OF RHODES

The alliance with Ptolemy was very profitable for Rhodes, but in 305 BCE it led the island into trouble. Ptolemy got into a quarrel with the king of Macedon, who sent his son Demetrius to attack Rhodes in order to prevent Ptolemy from using it as a military base. Demetrius sailed there with a massive force of 350 ships and 40,000 soldiers. His equipment included a forty-metre-high tower with nine floors, fitted with weapons and armour that was designed to break through the city's walls.

For a whole year, Demetrius attacked Rhodes without success. In the end, he had to admit defeat. He sailed away from the island, leaving behind the tower and all its armour. The people of Rhodes believed their victory was thanks to the patron god of their island, Helios, the Greek god of the Sun.

Deciding to build a giant statue in the god's honour, they stripped the bronze from Demetrius's tower and used it as the material for the Colossus of Rhodes. They displayed the statue in the harbour where Demetrius had launched his unsuccessful attack. And now's your chance to go back and see this immense statue up close!

SURVIVE IN TIME

We're going to be travelling to 250 BCE. There shouldn't be any enemy soldiers, angry workmen or hungry mummies wandering around on this day, so there's a good chance you'll get through this trip without being chased, imprisoned or eaten.

Rhodes was – and still is – a fascinating city, and there'll be lots to see and do. Since it was a well-known centre of Greek learning, with schools teaching philosophy and science, you have two missions for this trip: visit the Colossus of Rhodes and meet a famous philosopher.

Here's your AI translator and your special watch in the unlikely event you find yourself trapped in some deep and inescapable peril. Good luck!

***

The time machine drops you in the central marketplace of the city, or agora as it's called in ancient Greek. There's a busy scene around you: shops selling food, drink, pottery and fabric; entertainers singing songs and telling stories; shoppers eating and chatting; children playing games. There are also fountains splashing with water, statues of Greek gods and goddesses, and lots of decorative columns. If there's one thing you've learned on these expeditions, it's that the ancient world really *liked* columns. They're everywhere!

I know what this city needs!

BRAND NEW COLUMN

Nobody notices you as you step out in your usual Greek clothing. Their attention is focused on the far end of the square. The men are all heading off in that direction, leaving the women and children behind. You guess this is another of those events that only men are allowed to attend. You decide to follow, hiding behind a particularly tall man so you don't get spotted.

You find yourself in another square with an impressive marble building at one end. Someone is climbing on to a stone platform, holding his arms out to quieten the gathering crowd. The men you've been following hurry forward to listen to what the speaker has to say, and the noise in the square dies down to a murmur. Could this be a famous philosopher? If so, this might just be your quickest mission yet! Are you going to listen to the speaker or find someone a bit less busy in one of the city's philosophy schools?

OPTION 1:
LISTEN TO THE SPEAKER
(PAGE 135)

OPTION 2:
LOOK FOR A SCHOOL OF
PHILOSOPHY (PAGE 138)

YOU DECIDE TO LISTEN TO THE SPEAKER.

You can't get close enough to hear what the man is talking about because children are not allowed in this part of the agora. This is a venue for adult males only. But from your hiding place in the shadows, your translator manages to catch a few words: law, important, trade, future, alliance. The speaker is very passionate. He waves his arms around and then clasps his hands together before the crowd, as though begging for their support. Some men shout out their agreement, while others seem less happy. They shake their heads or even wave their fists.

PERSON 1:
Wow, the speaker's so passionate! He's waving his arms everywhere!

PERSON 2:
There's a wasp on his nose.

The speech ends and another man climbs on to the stage. He reads from a scroll in a loud voice and announces: 'Cast your vote.' There is murmured discussion between groups of friends before people begin to move forward towards the stage. You can see two boxes: one marked YES and the other marked NO. Each voter carries one small token, which they place in one of the two boxes.

The man waits for everyone to finish before emptying the boxes. He and some other men begin to count the tokens while the speaker looks on anxiously.

Finally they're done and the man with the scroll steps forward. 'The law is passed.'

The speaker returns to the centre of the stage and bows before the crowd, some of whom are cheering and some who look bitterly disappointed. You've just witnessed a vote in the one of the world's first ever democracies!

That was fascinating! However, it does mean the speaker was a politician and not a philosopher. Time to move on. You wonder if you should ask someone for directions to a philosophy school and notice the tall man about to leave. But he might be angry that you sneaked into the voting assembly. Do you think you ought to look for a school yourself?

OPTION 1:
LOOK FOR A SCHOOL OF
PHILOSOPHY (PAGE 138)

OPTION 2:
ASK THE TALL MAN FOR
DIRECTIONS (PAGE 141)

THE BIRTH OF DEMOCRACY

A democracy is a political system invented by the ancient Greeks that allowed men to vote on the laws and leaders that governed their city. The idea of democracy was born in Athens in 508 BCE. Before this, Athens was ruled by kings, and then by a few rich people who made all the decisions. But many people didn't think this was fair. A leader named Cleisthenes wanted to give everyone a say, so he created a new system where citizens could vote on important issues that affected them. This was called democracy, which means 'rule by the people'. It wasn't like democracy today because women couldn't vote, but thanks to Cleisthenes, ordinary people, not just the rich or powerful, could now help decide how their city was run. Nice work! In Rhodes, things were not quite like Athens, since the richest families still held most of the power. But some laws were still decided by voting, as you just saw.

YOU DECIDE TO LOOK FOR A SCHOOL OF PHILOSOPHY.

You make your way along a narrow street with stone houses on both sides. Through a doorway, you hear the sound of laughter and spot a pair of children, a boy and a girl, playing together on the floor. They see you at the same moment and wave.

'Hey, want to play Fly?'

You've no idea what that means, but it sounds fun. 'Er . . . sure. What's Fly?'

They laugh incredulously. 'You don't know what Fly is?'

They explain it's a game in which one person puts on a blindfold and has to catch the others, who buzz around like flies. It's been a while since you've played like a normal kid, and it feels like a nice break from climbing through tombs and being bribed by spies, so you happily agree to join. The girl goes first, chasing you and the boy around the small room until she catches you with a triumphant cheer.

'Now your turn!'

You put on the blindfold and creep forward as the brother and sister dance around you. You can't see a thing and crash helplessly into a table, bringing peals of delighted laughter. It takes a while to get used to the dark, but finally you start to move more confidently. When you hear a noise in front of you, you jump forward and reach out with your hands.

'Got you, fly!' you shout as you make contact.

There's no reply, only a stunned silence, like if someone lets off a big fart in class and nobody knows whether it's OK to laugh or not. With a feeling of dread, you slowly peel off the blindfold and find yourself facing a very tall, frowning man. It's the man from the agora and he doesn't look friendly.

'I am NOT a fly,' he barks. 'But I am the father of these children. Who are you and what are you doing here?'

Who said you couldn't get into trouble in Rhodes?

'Quickly, child! I need to get back to the agora.'

You need to make a decision fast. Do you make an escape by activating your watch or explain you need directions to a philosophy school?

OPTION 1:
ACTIVATE YOUR SPECIAL WATCH (PAGE 158)

OPTION 2:
ASK THE TALL MAN FOR DIRECTIONS (PAGE 141)

HOW TO BE A KID IN ANCIENT GREECE

Boys and girls were brought up differently in Greece. Girls were usually educated by their mums, who taught them how to cook, sew and weave cloth for their work in the home. Boys went to school to learn to read and write, but only if their families could afford it (there were no free schools). They wrote on wax tablets, copying out famous Greek poems, and calculated sums with an abacus. In their free time, they played games like Fly, and also had simple toys such as spinning tops, balls and figurines.

YOU DECIDE TO ASK THE TALL MAN FOR DIRECTIONS.

He actually looks more puzzled than angry as he explains the way to the Academy of Rhodes. 'I doubt you'll understand a word they tell you,' he scoffs.

How dare he suggest you're not intelligent enough to study ancient Greek philosophy! Determined to prove him wrong, you follow his directions and find yourself in a leafy courtyard surrounded by rooms with desks and chairs. A man with straggly brown hair catches sight of you as he appears in one of the doorways.

'Welcome, child! Have you come to unravel the mysteries of consciousness? To delve into the unfathomable depths of human existence? To explore the boundless realms of reality and perception?'

You didn't understand a word of that and whisper to your AI device: 'Can you translate?'

'I think he said hello,' the machine replies.

'Er . . . is there a famous philosopher here?' you answer.

The man doesn't look like a famous philosopher. He doesn't have a long white beard, and everybody knows philosophers have long white beards. But hopefully he can help you find one.

'Famous? What is fame but a mirage of ego; a siren's song whispering seduction but delivering only disappointment?' comes the reply.

'Don't ask me,' says your AI device.

'Is there someone else here I can talk to? Someone who's a bit less –' Strange. '– busy.'

'Ah, to be considered busy! Such a peculiar and unwarranted accolade! How often we mistake busyness for purpose and confuse industry with meaningful endeavour!'

You and the AI are completely stumped by this point. Maybe you really aren't clever enough to understand Greek philosophy. But just as you're about to give up and walk out, you notice a sign on the wall:

PUBLIC LECTURE
'On the Nature of the Earth and Sun'
Academy of Rhodes
NOON TODAY

That sounds promising! Maybe the lecture is by a famous philosopher. Should you stick around for it or change paths and head for the Colossus of Rhodes by the sea?

OPTION 1:
ATTEND THE PUBLIC LECTURE (PAGE 146)

OPTION 2:
HEAD FOR THE COLOSSUS OF RHODES (PAGE 144)

GREEK PHILOSOPHY

The Greeks were really fond of thinking about stuff. The first Greek philosopher is considered to be Thales of Miletus, who was born around 624 BCE. Thales spent a lot of time trying to work out how the world was formed. He decided the Earth must be a flat disc floating on a vast sea. This was totally wrong, of course, but his desire to understand the world inspired many philosophers who came after him. One of the most famous thinkers was Socrates of Athens. Socrates came up with a new method of teaching that involved asking people lots of questions to make them think about stuff in new ways. Socrates was very clever, but unfortunately his method embarrassed people, especially those in powerful positions. Eventually the leaders of Athens got so angry they forced him to drink poison. (Disclaimer: I'm not recommending you do this to teachers who ask you difficult questions.)

YOU DECIDE TO HEAD FOR THE COLOSSUS OF RHODES.

You don't need to ask for directions to the sea, as a quick sniff brings the strong aroma of fish. You follow the odour down a wide street, which soon opens up into one of the two harbours of Rhodes.

You see a fresh catch being taken off one of the many wooden boats, and a group of bare-chested sailors are hurrying to get the load on shore. The ship's captain, a grizzled veteran with a craggy face and a thick black beard, shouts at them to get a move on.

'Come on – we haven't got all day! Quick, before the fish start to rot!'

You don't really want to be around rotting fish, so you start to back away, your eyes searching for the Colossus. There's no sign of it and you start to wonder if you're in the wrong harbour. But the captain has spotted you loitering and yells out: 'Hey, you, child! Come here! Want to earn a coin?'

Thanks to the pilot's stinginess, you've never owned

After you've visited the Colossus, how about trying our famous rotting fish? The best in Greece!

a Greek coin before and you wonder what you could buy with it. How much does a pair of trainers cost in ancient Greece? They would certainly be comfier than these rock-hard sandals you've been running around in this whole time!

'I had a guest on my ship, but he forgot one of his cases,' the captain says. 'He's staying at the inn on the other side of the bay. You can have a bronze coin if you take his case to him.'

Your stomach is rumbling and your feet are burning, and the bronze coin is sounding very tempting right now. You're thinking about whether to take on the task when you notice a piece of paper blowing along the ground. You pick it up and find the same notice you saw at the Academy.

OPTION 1:
TAKE THE CASE TO THE GUEST (PAGE 148)

OPTION 2:
ATTEND THE PUBLIC LECTURE (PAGE 146)

YOU DECIDE TO ATTEND THE PUBLIC LECTURE.

You're not sure how long you're going to need to wait because your special watch doesn't actually have a clock, but you find the lecture room in the Academy and sit down. It's a plain white room without any of the bright posters or terrible student paintings of fruit bowls that decorate your own classroom at school. There is, however, a scroll on the desk and you open it up carefully, wondering what it's about. Your device translates the ancient Greek title: *On the Sizes and Distances of the Sun and Moon by Aristarchus of Samos*. Inside, you find complicated mathematical drawings of Earth and its position in relation to the Moon and the Sun.

You can't follow the calculations beneath the drawings, but you do understand one thing: this is not a book of philosophy, or what you thought philosophy was, but of science. Aristarchus has noted down what he has seen in the sky to make predictions about the solar system. You can't tell if his predictions are right or not, but using what you see to draw conclusions about the world is the same method scientists still use today!

'There's that rude child from before, trying to steal a scroll!'

You look up to see the straggly-haired man pointing at you angrily. Next to him is a younger colleague. No white beard on him either; just an even messier mop of hair.

'I'm not stealing! I'm just waiting for the lecture so I can meet a famous philosopher.'

The man wags his finger. 'I already gave you a very straightforward explanation about the nature of fame. What more could you want?'

'Ah, fame,' his colleague remarks. 'What is fame but the sad illusion of self-worth?'

'Exactly what I said! This ignorant child is obviously not here for the lecture. Let's report the thief to the authorities.'

You have a second to decide what to do. Activate your watch or try to run straight to the Colossus.

OPTION 1:
ACTIVATE YOUR SPECIAL
WATCH (PAGE 158)

OPTION 2:
RUN STRAIGHT
TO THE COLOSSUS
(PAGE 151)

YOU DECIDE TO TAKE THE CASE TO THE GUEST.

The inn is a large stone building with stables attached for horses. There's a scattering of travellers inside munching on simple meals of bread, olives and cheese. You stroll up to the bar with the case and ask the innkeeper if any new guests have just arrived. The innkeeper points to an old man drinking wine by himself in the corner. He has a large bald forehead and a long white beard. And we all know who have long white beards . . .

'Excuse me. You're not a philosopher by any chance, are you?' you blurt out.

The old man spits out a mouthful of red wine, which goes all over his beard. 'How could you possibly know that?' he exclaims. 'Oh, you've brought me my case! I knew I'd forgotten something!'

You hand him the case and he introduces himself. 'My name is Aristarchus of Samos and, yes, I am a philosopher. I study the heavens and try to understand what I'm observing. For example, most people believe the Earth is at the centre of the universe and our Sun revolves around it. But my observations lead me to believe it's the opposite. The Sun is the larger body, and we revolve around it. Unfortunately my view isn't a popular one.' He takes a long gulp of wine.

'You're right and they're wrong,' you state confidently. 'I learned it at school.'

Another mouthful of wine spurts out from Aristarchus's mouth and splatters your tunic. 'How extraordinary,' he exclaims. 'I'll have to mention that at my lecture later!'

Just then, your watch starts to flash: a message from the pilot to say you don't have much time. What should you do? If you quickly return to the captain to collect your coin, you'll make your money, but will you have time to see the Colossus of Rhodes too? Or should you run straight to the Colossus in the other harbour?

OPTION 1:
RETURN TO COLLECT YOUR COIN (PAGE 155)

OPTION 2:
RUN STRAIGHT TO THE COLOSSUS (PAGE 151)

ARISTARCHUS OF SAMOS

Aristarchus of Samos is not as famous today as such philosophers as Socrates or Aristotle. However, he seems to have been the first person to realize that Earth revolves around the Sun rather than the other way around. This might seem like common sense to us today, but Aristarchus's theory was so unbelievable to people that it was almost 2,000 years before they began to accept it. He was a genius! And do you want to know something else about him? He really did have a long white beard.

ARISTARCHUS:
If you had to wait 2,000 years for people to believe you, your beard would be white too.

YOU DECIDE TO RUN STRAIGHT TO THE COLOSSUS.

You go as fast as you can, dashing past fishing boats as they unload their catches. Wafts of recently caught fish float through the air. *Do people ever get used to the smell?* you wonder. You're keeping your eyes peeled for a glimpse of the Colossus when you suddenly hear a shout of warning from one of the boats.

'Watch out! Don't step on that –' you feel your foot land on something wet and slippery, and your leg suddenly disappears from under you – 'fish.'

You do a half-flip in the air, like a cartoon character slipping on a banana peel, and tumble helplessly off the edge of the harbour. You land in a boat and your head hits the deck with a resounding thud. Everything goes black.

The first thing you notice when you wake up is the immense pain in your head. It feels as though someone is hitting you from each side with a heavy mallet. The second thing you notice is blue sea. Lots and lots of blue sea.

'Oh good, you're awake! Feeling OK?' A fisherman is standing over you with a concerned expression. 'Sorry, we had to set off. But don't worry, this isn't a long trip. We'll be back in a week.'

'*A week?*' You groan in horror.

'Just enough time for you to get used to the life of a fisherman. Hope you like the smell of fish!'

You let out another groan. *Now what?* Will the pilot wait a week for you to come back from the fishing trip and complete your mission?

OPTION 1:
ACTIVATE YOUR SPECIAL WATCH (PAGE 158)

OPTION 2:
STAY ON THE FISHING BOAT FOR A WEEK (PAGE 154)

THINGS THE GREEKS GOT WRONG

Those clever Greek philosophers didn't get everything right. Here are four things they believed that we now know to be completely false:

1. Flies are born by magically appearing in old meat. Nope! They come from tiny eggs that are too small to see. (Still disgusting, but at least it's true.)

2. Everything is made of just earth, air, fire, and water. If that were true, then how do you explain the existence of cheesy hotdogs?

3. Your brain's job is to cool down your body, and your heart does all the thinking. Try using your heart to answer questions on your next school test and let me know how you get on . . .

4. Women get ill because their womb wanders around their body like a lost hiker. This one is just SILLY.

OH DEAR, NOT THE SMARTEST CHOICE.

By the time you get back from your trip, the pilot has long gone. Besides, he wouldn't have let you into the time machine smelling that strongly of fish. But wipe those tears away! The following letter will be provided to anyone interested in your whereabouts:

Dear parent, guardian, teacher or interested person,

It is with great regret that we inform you of the loss of [insert name here] in Rhodes. It appears they failed to return to the transport vehicle by the scheduled time. Although at this point it is difficult to know where (or when) they are, we can assure you we are doing everything in our power to find them.

Please be aware that [insert name here] was clearly warned of the risks involved with their journey. The company cannot, therefore, take any financial responsibility for their disappearance.

Yours sincerely,

Intrepid Explorers Inc.

Think you could do better next time?
Go back and start again on page 132!

YOU DECIDE TO RETURN TO COLLECT YOUR COIN.

You wish Aristarchus luck with his lecture and run back to the captain, who gives you the bronze coin with thanks. You're holding an object that's more than 2,250 years old. What an amazing thing to bring back to your own time! You start to daydream again about selling the coin and building that chocolate house you've always wanted. But your watch flashes a warning once more.

'I don't have time to get to the Colossus!' you exclaim.

'The Colossus, you say?'

You turn to see a fisherman about to pull off from the shore in a small boat. 'I'll be passing the Colossus on my way. I can drop you there if you want.'

You can't believe your luck. 'Really? Thanks!'

'No problem. I'll just ask for a *chalkous* for my trouble.'

'A *chalkous*? What's that?'

The man frowns. 'The coin, of course.'

So much for the chocolate house. You hand it over with a sigh and get in the fisherman's boat, which he zips across the water. With the wind whipping through your hair, you soon forget your disappointment and enjoy the ride as the little boat cuts through the waves. Before you know it, you've rounded the bay and entered another harbour. There in front of you is the biggest and most impressive statue you've ever seen in your life.

It's a giant figure of gleaming bronze standing on a white marble base: the Greek god of the Sun, Helios. It's thirty-three metres in height, like three buses stacked end to end. The great god is naked except for a bronze cloak on his back, and his legs and chest are carved with enormous muscles. One of his arms is raised in the air, as though welcoming people to Rhodes, and a crown of spikes on his head represent the fiery rays of the Sun. It's a magnificent sight, enough to take your breath away.

'I can drop you here if you like,' says the fisherman. 'But judging by the smile on your face, you look like you have a good head for the sea. I could do with a young apprentice if you want to join me.'

You think about the many dangers you've faced during your last few journeys and wonder if a more peaceful life at sea might be the easier choice.

OPTION 1:
JOIN THE FISHERMAN AS
AN APPRENTICE
(PAGE 154)

OPTION 2:
RETURN TO THE TIME
MACHINE (PAGE 159)

THE START AND END
OF THE COLOSSUS

The Colossus was sculpted by an artist named
Chares, who melted the bronze from Demetrius's
tower and moulded it into new shapes. He built the
Colossus from the ground up, filling the legs with stones
so they'd be heavy enough to hold the weight of the
upper body. Sadly the statue didn't stand for long. In
about 226 BCE, an earthquake sent it toppling to the
ground. In the fall, the great sections of the body split
apart. For more than 800 years, it lay in pieces on the
ground. But in 654 CE, Rhodes was conquered by Arabs
from Syria. They stripped the bronze from the fallen
statue and melted it down to be sold.

YOU ACTIVATE YOUR SPECIAL WATCH AND RETURN TO THE TIME MACHINE.

Unfortunately you didn't manage to complete your mission of meeting a famous philosopher and visiting the Colossus of Rhodes.

'I actually thought you'd get through that one unharmed,' the pilot says. 'You have a real knack for getting yourself in slippery situations.'

'Just a natural gift, I guess.'

'Oh well, the next mission is to the Lighthouse of Alexandria. Even you should be able to spot a lighthouse without bother.'

Feeling brave enough to give it another try?
Go back to page 132!

CONGRATULATIONS! YOU COMPLETED YOUR MISSION!

You met a famous philosopher and visited the Colossus of Rhodes. The pilot holds out his hand as you step into the time machine, and you see a small coin in his palm.

'You got my bronze coin back!' you exclaim.

It's the first nice thing he's done for you, and a grateful tear springs to your eye.

'Don't get used to it,' he says. 'Anyway, we'd better set off. We're going to the Lighthouse of Alexandria next.'

CHAPTER 6:
THE LIGHTHOUSE OF ALEXANDRIA

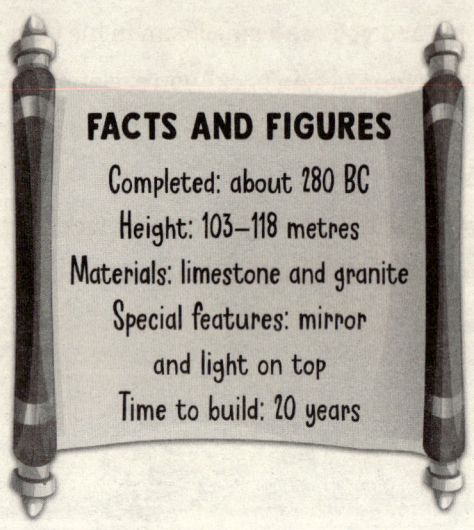

FACTS AND FIGURES

Completed: about 280 BC

Height: 103–118 metres

Materials: limestone and granite

Special features: mirror
and light on top

Time to build: 20 years

WELCOME TO ALEXANDRIA!

It's time to talk about Alexander the Great again. In his short
career as a professional conqueror, the young Macedonian
king took over Greece, Turkey, Syria, Mesopotamia, Persia and
Egypt. Egypt had at that point been part of the Persian Empire
and its capital city had been Memphis. But after his conquest,
Alexander decided to create a new capital of Egypt, further
north on the coast of the Mediterranean Sea. He built the city
entirely from scratch and named it Alexandria after himself.
He was modest like that.

BEST ALEXANDRIA OF THEM ALL

Alexandria wasn't the only city Alexander the Great established. In fact, he created as many as twenty, and at least seven of them were called Alexandria. It must have been a nightmare for messengers trying to deliver letters.

WOMAN:
You've got the wrong Alexandria.
Try the one in Persia.

MESSENGER:
They told me to try
this Alexandra!

Thanks to its location on the Mediterranean Sea, Alexandria in Egypt linked Europe with Africa, and became one of the richest and most important cities in the world. Although Alexander himself never saw it after it was built (he was far too busy conquering and stuff), it turned into a thriving hub of trade and culture. Ships sailed in and out of its great harbour with goods from all over the world, and architects competed to design the most magnificent temples, theatres and palaces for its wide streets. It was particularly famous for its library, which collected books from all over the world, and, of course, for its lighthouse, one of the Seven Wonders of the Ancient World.

The construction of the lighthouse was started by Ptolemy I in around 300 BCE (yes, the same Ptolemy who made that alliance with Rhodes and got the island into trouble with

Demetrius of Macedon – well remembered!). The purpose of the lighthouse was to warn ships of the treacherous reefs around the port.

MOST FAMOUS QUEEN EVER

For our next trip, we're going to visit Alexandria when one of its most famous figures was in charge – Queen Cleopatra VII. She was the last ruler of Egypt before it was taken over by the Roman Empire in 30 BCE. The first thing to know about Cleopatra is that she wasn't Egyptian but Macedonian. She was the daughter of King Ptolemy XII, a descendant of Ptolemy I. Unlike the rest of the royal family, however, Cleopatra took the trouble to learn Egyptian so she could communicate with her subjects. She could also speak at least eight other languages, including Greek, Latin, Hebrew, Arabic and Ethiopian. She was a real clever clogs!

A TRAGIC LOVE STORY

Cleopatra became queen at the age of eighteen after the death of her father. But after a year, she was driven out of Egypt by supporters of her ten-year-old brother, even though he couldn't speak Egyptian – or even make his own breakfast in the morning.

Looking for help to get her throne back, Cleopatra met

with the great Roman general Julius Caesar, who was fighting in the region. Caesar was blown away by the queen's intelligence and beauty, and agreed to join forces. They soon fell in love and Cleopatra gave birth to their baby boy.

With Caesar's help, Cleopatra defeated her brother in battle and regained her throne. But shortly afterwards, Caesar was murdered in Rome by his enemies, who felt he was becoming too powerful.

The general's death left Rome with two rivals for power: Caesar's friend Mark Antony and Caesar's nephew Octavian. Cleopatra knew she needed the support of the Romans to keep her position as queen secure, so she met with Mark Antony in Turkey. The two fell deeply in love and had three children together, two boys and a girl.

Unfortunately their love couldn't last.

In 31 BCE, they fought against Octavian in a sea battle at Actium near Greece. Octavian won an overwhelming victory and followed Cleopatra and Antony back to Alexandria. As Antony went off to fight one last battle, Cleopatra locked herself away in the royal palace, praying he wouldn't be defeated. But Antony lost. Badly wounded, he took himself back to the palace, where he died in Cleopatra's arms. The Egyptian queen was left with no one to protect her and her enemy Octavian on his way . . .

SURVIVE IN TIME

Today we're going to Alexandria in the year 30 BCE. It's an important moment in history because it's just after Antony has been defeated by Octavian. Cleopatra is all alone in her royal palace, having sent her children away from Egypt to try to keep them safe. Octavian is on his way to the palace to take her prisoner.

You have two missions: explore the top of the Lighthouse of Alexandria and try to help Queen Cleopatra. Along with your AI translator, I'm giving you an unusual piece of equipment for this expedition: a pot of glue. It isn't modern glue, but the same kind the ancient Egyptians used themselves. You can keep it in a small bag on your shoulder, but I'll leave it up to you to decide how and when to use it. Try not to get into any 'sticky' situations! Ha ha!

***

You start your expedition outside the Library of Alexandria, which is halfway between the royal palace and the lighthouse. It's an impressive building of stone and marble with a grand doorway flanked by beautifully carved pillars.

It's late afternoon and the air is hot and dusty. You're sweating buckets. You hear a babble of voices that your AI translator finds difficult to pick up because they're all speaking different languages. Alexandria is a multicultural city, with Greeks, Egyptians, Romans, Jews, Ethiopians, Nubians, Syrians and many other people all living side by side. Greek is the official language of the city, but there are lots of other languages being spoken too.

When you look more closely at the passers-by, you see different skin colours, hairstyles and clothing. Some men are bare-chested, with skirts around their waists and sandals on their feet. Some women wear long dresses and jewellery made from coloured stones. Other people are in Greek-style tunics and dresses. Some men have long beards, and some are clean shaven. Some women have long, flowing hair while others have veils covering their heads. It's a magnificent melting pot of so many different cultures, languages, styles and beliefs.

It's time to focus on your mission now. You could go to the royal palace to find Cleopatra, though you can't imagine how on earth a strange, time-travelling child from the future could possibly help a great Egyptian queen. Or you could head for the Lighthouse of Alexandria.

OPTION 1:
HEAD FOR THE ROYAL PALACE (PAGE 166)

OPTION 2:
HEAD FOR THE LIGHTHOUSE (PAGE 168)

YOU DECIDE TO HEAD FOR THE ROYAL PALACE.

The streets of Alexandria are set out in a grid pattern, so it's not hard to find your way around. You guess the palace will be close to the sea, where a refreshing breeze blows through the humid city.

Dusty from the streets, you find yourself at one end of a giant harbour full of ships. Huge numbers of men are working on the docks, loading the ships with grain and fruit. Many of the boats are headed to Rome. Egypt is known as the 'breadbasket of Rome' because so much of the city's grain is grown here.

On a strip of land extending out into the sea, you see a collection of lavish buildings surrounded by high white walls: the royal palace and gardens. You set off to take a closer look, only to be stopped at the gate by a pair of tall and imposing soldiers. They're holding shields and spears, and are wearing iron helmets and breastplates above red tunics. They look just like they do in the history books – legionaries from the Roman army!

'This is a restricted area, you smelly urchin! Clear off!' shouts one of the legionaries.

Smelly? How dare he! You took a shower in the time machine after visiting the Great Pyramid of Giza, just 1,970 years ago!

OPTION 1:
HEAD FOR THE
LIGHTHOUSE (PAGE 168)

OPTION 2:
EXPLAIN YOUR MISSION
TO THE LEGIONARY
(PAGE 173)

THE ROMAN LEGIONS

The Roman legions were the mighty army of ancient Rome, known for their strength and discipline. A legion consisted of about 5,000 men, all trained to fight together like a powerful machine. Each soldier, called a legionary, wore shiny armour, carried a large shield and used a spear and short sword as weapons. They were famous for marching long distances and using clever tactics to win battles, even when they were massively outnumbered. In 52 BCE, for example, Julius Caesar needed just 60,000 men to defeat an army of 250,000 warriors from Gaul (modern-day France). The legions didn't just fight; they also built roads, forts and bridges, helping to spread Roman culture all over Europe, North Africa and the Middle East.

YOU DECIDE TO HEAD FOR THE LIGHTHOUSE.

Alexandria is a big city, but you don't need a map to tell you that the lighthouse will be by the sea.

The harbour is packed with ships of every size. On one side are the white walls of the royal palace gardens, while on the other is your destination: an island with a great lighthouse at one end. There's a mile-long causeway to reach the island and you hurry along it, sweating in the heat. The island is called Pharos and it's guarded by a large fort. Luckily the fort doesn't seem to be occupied right now, and you skip past it towards the lighthouse. This is too easy!

It doesn't look like any other lighthouse you've seen

Running a mile in sweltering heat on an empty stomach? What a great start!

before. Instead of a smooth, round tower, it has three separate sections, with the widest at the bottom and the narrowest at the top. The bottom section is square in shape; the one in the middle is octagonal; and the top one is rounded. On the peak is a statue of a Greek god. You're not sure if it's Zeus, the king of the gods, or Poseidon, the ruler of the seas. Altogether, the structure is more than a hundred metres tall, far higher than anything else in the city.

To get to the top, you'll have to go inside, but the thick wooden door at the base is firmly locked. As you contemplate your options, you notice a pair of workers coming towards you, wheeling two carts piled high with wood. They have bare chests with skirts around their waist in the Egyptian style. Should you speak to them, or try a sneakier way to get into the lighthouse?

OPTION 1:
HIDE IN ONE OF THE
CARTS (PAGE 180)

OPTION 2:
SPEAK TO THE EGYPTIANS
(PAGE 170)

YOU DECIDE TO SPEAK TO THE EGYPTIANS.

They take their carts to the base of the lighthouse, and the larger of the pair produces an iron key to unlock the thick wooden door. He pulls it open to reveal a staircase winding upward into the darkness. You keep to one side as the men begin to unload the wood from the cart and wait for the right opportunity to speak to them.

'We'll be taking orders from the Romans soon,' you hear the larger man grumble. 'The rumour is the queen has already been captured by Octavian.'

His friend shakes his head unhappily. 'Cleopatra was a good ruler. She cared for us Egyptians – even learned our language. How many of the other Ptolemies did that?'

'None! She deserves better than to end her days as a prisoner of the Romans.'

The men fall silent as they return to their task. 'Come on, let's get the lighthouse lit. It'll be dark soon.'

This is your only chance to get inside. You jump out from your

I guess we should start climbing these 400 steps then.

Yeah . . . or we could just keep talking?

hiding place and politely ask the men if they need your help. They shake their heads firmly.

'You can't enter the lighthouse without authorization.'

'And how do I get that?'

A shrug. 'The royal palace usually. But now the Romans have taken over, who knows? Maybe you'll have to talk to Octavian.'

You need to decide who to try to get permission from – the captured queen or the new Roman ruler?

OPTION 1:
SEEK PERMISSION FROM
CLEOPATRA (PAGE 178)

OPTION 2:
SEEK PERMISSION FROM
OCTAVIAN (PAGE 176)

THE LIGHTHOUSE OF ALEXANDRIA

The lighthouse was built long before the invention of electric light bulbs. So, how did it shine at night? The answer is it had a giant mirror and a fire at the top. When the fire was lit, the mirror reflected its light out to sea, allowing it to be seen by ships from far and wide. How clever! It did this important job for more than 1,500 years until it was damaged by a series of earthquakes and eventually crumbled away.

WORKER 1:
Stop posing in front of the mirror!

WORKER 2:
But how will the ships see my muscles?

YOU DECIDE TO EXPLAIN YOUR MISSION TO THE LEGIONARY.

He looks at you like a lion might regard a Chihuahua who's just challenged it to a fight: with a mixture of amusement and contempt.

'I really want to help Cleopatra!' you explain. 'She needs me to . . . er . . .'

The soldier pulls the bag from your shoulder and looks inside. 'Glue something?'

He pauses, seemingly weighing up whether to continue the conversation or just pick you up and throw you in the sea. You wait nervously for him to make up his mind.

'Let's take you to see Octavian,' he says at last. 'He'll know what to do with you.'

Grabbing you by the arm, he drags you into the palace gardens, where you find a slender young man in a military uniform accompanied by a troop of soldiers. He has blond hair with small curls and blue eyes that shine with intelligence. He frowns as you approach.

'You brought me a street urchin, centurion. How thoughtful.'

The legionary hangs his head in embarrassment. 'Forgive me, Imperator. It asked to be let into the royal palace, and claims to be on a mission to help the queen.'

The young man raises his eyebrows. 'Helping the queen would make you my enemy, child. My name is Gaius Octavius, and Cleopatra is about to become my prisoner.'

'The urchin's going to stop you with his glue!' mocks the centurion.

Baffled, Octavian turns back to you. 'I must go to the palace now, but we'll speak again when I return. Centurion, this child is not to be harmed. Give it some food and –' he looks you up and down – 'perhaps a bath.'

Oh no! Is this adventure over before it's even begun? Should you head back to the time machine before you get yourself into danger, or wait for Octavian to return and hope he gives you permission to enter the lighthouse?

Any other 'dangerous' prisoners for me, centurion?

Well, actually . . .

OPTION 1:
ACTIVATE YOUR SPECIAL WATCH (PAGE 188)

OPTION 2:
WAIT FOR OCTAVIAN TO RETURN (PAGE 180)

THE GREATNESS
OF OCTAVIAN

Octavian was not a bad man. In fact,
he became the greatest leader in all of
Rome's history. After he returned
home from Egypt, he was asked to
become the supreme ruler of Rome.
Soon he was given the title of emperor
and became known as Emperor
Augustus. He ruled for an incredible
forty-one years, and under his
guidance the city became peaceful and
rich. He constructed many fine
buildings, including temples, roads and
bridges, and expanded Rome's empire
with the help of its powerful legions.

YOU DECIDE TO SEEK PERMISSION FROM OCTAVIAN.

You're not sure where in the city he'll be, so your plan is to approach the first group of Roman soldiers you find and ask them to take you to him. Luckily you don't have to go far. On the other side of the island of Pharos, you find what appears to be a military camp. Surrounded by a large ditch with a wall of wooden stakes behind it, it's guarded by red-cloaked men in metal helmets: Roman soldiers. You head to a gate at the front, where they are standing with spears and shields.

'I need to see Octavian!' you announce confidently.

One of the guards salutes you. 'Of course! We'll send for him right away!'

Wow, that was easy! 'Really?'

'No. Go away, you dirty little urchin.'

'But I need his permission to get into the lighthouse.'

The soldier sighs. 'Look, kid, we couldn't take you to Octavian even if we wanted to – which we don't. We're from Mark Antony's legions. We don't even know what Octavian is going to do to us yet.' He glances at his comrades uneasily. 'If you want to wait for him, you can sit out there. He'll be here eventually to tell us what our fate is.'

OPTION 1:
SEEK PERMISSION FROM
CLEOPATRA (PAGE 178)

OPTION 2:
WAIT FOR OCTAVIAN TO
ARRIVE (PAGE 180)

MARK ANTONY'S LEGIONS

The civil war between Antony and Octavian was hard for Roman soldiers, who were divided into legions of around 5,000 men. Some legions had been commanded by Antony for many years, and they felt loyal to him as their general. But in the civil war, they had to fight against other Roman legions led by Octavian. When Octavian was victorious, they must have worried about what would happen to them. Fortunately however, Octavian didn't punish them – he placed the soldiers into his own legions so they could fight for him and Rome.

YOU DECIDE TO SEEK PERMISSION FROM CLEOPATRA.

You walk towards the palace gate, where there are Roman soldiers guarding it at every corner. To keep out of their sight, you realize the only way in is to climb over the wall into the garden. It's a very dangerous move, but didn't you do something similar in Babylon? It worked out OK then, except for being chased by a guard with a huge spear.

Stretching on to your tiptoes, you place your hands on top of the high white wall and heave yourself over. Dropping down on the other side behind a clump of trees, you're relieved to find no soldiers in sight. You're in an incredible garden with stone paths winding between exotic orchids and brightly flowering bushes. There are statues of Greek gods and goddesses as well as fountains that sprinkle the grass with cool water.

The royal palace is in front of you, a magnificent white building with a pair of huge wooden doors decorated on each side with sculptures of lions. You creep forward, keeping your head low until you get inside. You somehow make it through the door without being stopped and look up to see the most splendid room you've ever been in. The floor is made of white marble, and the walls are decorated with colourful mosaics. There are statues and vases everywhere, painted in gorgeous colours, and the ceiling, high above, is carved into flowing patterns. You take a step forward, only for a stern voice to call out behind you: 'Oi, where do you think you're going?'

You freeze at the sight of a big Roman soldier. 'Nowhere,' you offer weakly.

'You look like a smelly little spy to me.'

'I'm not a smelly little spy! I take . . . fairly regular baths!' you protest. Then you catch a glimpse of yourself in the polished marble floor. Your hair is matted with sweat and your legs covered in dust. 'Well, I'm not a spy anyway.'

OPTION 1:
MAKE A RUN FOR IT
(PAGE 181)

OPTION 2:
EXPLAIN YOUR MISSION
TO THE LEGIONARY
(PAGE 173)

BAD LUCK. YOU DON'T GET ANYWHERE DOING THAT.

It isn't long before you're discovered by one of Octavian's legionaries, who assumes that you're up to no good. He takes you away for questioning, and the pilot ends up leaving without you. But it's all right! The following letter will be provided to anyone interested in your whereabouts:

Dear parent, guardian, teacher or interested person,

It is with great regret that we inform you of the loss of [insert name here] in Alexandria. It appears they failed to return to the transport vehicle by the scheduled time. Although at this point it is difficult to know where (or when) they are, we can assure you we are doing everything in our power to find them.

Please be aware that [insert name here] was clearly warned of the risks involved with their journey. The company cannot, therefore, take any financial responsibility for their disappearance.

Yours sincerely,

Intrepid Explorers Inc.

Think you could do better next time?
Go back and start again on page 164!

YOU DECIDE TO MAKE A RUN FOR IT.

You dash away before the soldier can grab you, leaping up a flight of marble steps. You reach a long hallway, which ends in another staircase. You climb it without any idea of where you're going, and eventually emerge into another corridor. It's eerily quiet here.

Suddenly you hear a sound coming from behind a wooden door on your left. It sounds like a woman crying. Nervously you open the door a fraction and peer through the crack. In the room, you see a large bed with posts made of shining silver. Sitting on the edge is a black-haired lady wearing a white dress with a gold belt around the waist.

She jumps up, her eyes opening wide in alarm. 'Who are you? Are you with Octavian?'

'No, no!' You edge into the room slowly. 'Are you Queen Cleopatra? I . . . think I'm meant to help you.'

The lady stares at you, her expression still fearful. 'Help me how?'

'I don't know,' you confess sheepishly. 'I have some glue.'

Cleopatra lets out a sigh. 'I don't need glue. Besides, I don't think anyone can help me now.'

You apologize, feeling helpless.

'That's all right, little one,' she says kindly. She moves over to the window and looks outside, where darkness has begun to fall. Her face creases into a frown. 'That's strange.

The lighthouse hasn't been lit. The ships won't be warned of the reefs.'

A thought occurs to you. 'I could go check if you like. But I need permission to enter.'

Cleopatra smiles gently. 'I can give you permission. My final act as queen.'

She goes to a desk and uses a brush and ink to write out a parchment in Greek. 'You know, you remind me of my twins, Alexander and Selene. You have the same kindness in your eyes. I hope you can come back later. You'll find me on the bottom floor.'

She returns to her bed with a wistful expression, and you slip out of the room. You make your way back towards the palace entrance, where you stop dead in your tracks. There are a group of soldiers standing at the bottom. There's no escape this time.

OPTION 1:
SHOW CLEOPATRA'S LETTER TO THE SOLDIERS (PAGE 183)

OPTION 2:
ACTIVATE YOUR SPECIAL WATCH (PAGE 188)

YOU DECIDE TO SHOW CLEOPATRA'S LETTER TO THE SOLDIERS.
But before you even get a chance to utter a word, they march
straight past you and up the stairs, their expressions grim
behind their iron helmets. Barely giving you a glance, they
hurry off down the hallway, leaving you all alone. You worry
for Cleopatra. Are they heading to her chamber to take her
prisoner?

There's nothing you can do to stop them, and once again a
feeling of helplessness sweeps over you. Sighing, you climb
over the palace wall and head back to the lighthouse. You're
surprised to find the lighthouse door open this time, with no
sign of the two workers. You set off up the stairs, which wind
round in a never-ending spiral.

You're out of breath by the time you finally reach the top.
The two Egyptians are there and immediately order you to
leave. That is, until you show them the note from Cleopatra.

'Signed by the queen herself! You must be important.'

You shrug. 'She's wondering why the lighthouse isn't lit.'

That brings a withering look. 'The mirror's broken! We
don't know what to do!'

Sure enough, the great mirror that reflects the fire far out
to sea is in two pieces on the floor. By the guilty expression
on the smaller man's face, you suspect there's been an
unfortunate accident.

Suddenly everything becomes clear. You reach into your bag and produce the pot of glue. 'Will this help?'

The two Egyptians look at you as if you're a superhero. 'Yes, I think it might!' the larger one says with a grin.

Just then, your watch starts to flash. Time is running out. You've only completed half your mission by visiting the lighthouse. Do you have time to return to the palace to help Cleopatra too? With so many Roman soldiers around, it will surely be dangerous.

OPTION 1:
ACTIVATE YOUR SPECIAL WATCH (PAGE 188)

OPTION 2:
RETURN TO CLEOPATRA (PAGE 185)

YOU DECIDE TO RETURN TO CLEOPATRA.

There are lots of Roman soldiers around the palace now, and you have to be extra sneaky to get inside this time. Cleopatra told you she'd be on the bottom floor, so instead of going up the stairs, you head underground. You find yourself in a stone corridor lit by torches along the wall. It's deathly quiet, and your footsteps echo spookily. You're just thinking about turning around and heading to the time machine when something suddenly moves at your feet. You jump back in fright as you see a dark creature slithering across the floor. It's a snake!

You can't even scream in case there are any soldiers around, so you clasp your hand over your mouth as the creature slides away into the darkness. You turn to see where the snake had appeared from – a room at the end of the hall. Could this be where Queen Cleopatra is?

You head towards the room and find the queen lying back on a cushioned bench, touching her hand to her chest.

'I saw a snake!' you blurt out. 'It came from in here!'

Cleopatra beckons you over with a pale smile. 'You came back. I'm so glad.'

You look more closely at her in the dim light. There's a drop of blood on her chest.

'It bit you!' you exclaim in horror. 'We have to get you help! I'm going to call the soldiers! They can fetch a doctor!'

Cleopatra shushes you gently, touching her fingers to your lips. 'It's all right, child. The snake was *meant* to bite me.' She lets out a small gasp and for a moment her eyelids close. 'Tell me, did you check the lighthouse?'

'Yes, I did,' you reply quickly. 'The mirror was broken but I helped them fix it.'

'With your glue.' The queen lets out a soft laugh. 'Thank you, my child. Thank you for helping and for coming back to see me. You do so remind me of my twins.'

Her eyes close again and this time they don't open. Her hand drops from your face.

You can't help the tear that rolls down your cheek.

OPTION 1:
RETURN TO THE TIME
MACHINE (PAGE 189)

OPTION 2:
REMAIN WITH CLEOPATRA
(PAGE 180)

CLEOPATRA'S CHOICE

Cleopatra didn't want to be captured by Octavian and so, according to Roman historians, she let a poisonous snake bite her. She died in her mausoleum somewhere in the royal palace. To keep her children safe, the queen had sent them away from Egypt, but they were soon captured by Octavian. He had her eldest child killed (as the son of Julius Caesar, he could have become a dangerous rival), but he didn't harm her other three children. In fact, he helped her daughter, Selene, become a powerful queen in Mauretania in northern Africa. We'll never know what would have happened to Cleopatra if she'd been taken prisoner.

YOU ACTIVATE YOUR SPECIAL WATCH AND RETURN TO THE TIME MACHINE.

Unfortunately you didn't manage to complete your mission of reaching the top of the Lighthouse of Alexandria and helping Queen Cleopatra. You didn't even do anything silly – you just got a bit unlucky this time.

'It's the final trip next,' the pilot says, as you take your seat. 'We're going to the Temple of Artemis at Ephesus.'

He smiles at your blank look.

'It'll be fun. We'll be going there in 120 CE when the Romans are at their most powerful. You know what that means, don't you?'

You shake your head.

He can barely hold back his excitement. 'Crucifixion.'

Feeling brave enough to give it another try?
Go back to page 164!

CONGRATULATIONS! YOU COMPLETED YOUR MISSION!

You explored the top of the Lighthouse of Alexandria and helped Queen Cleopatra.

'That was very sad. I don't feel like I helped Cleopatra at all,' you complain as you enter the time machine. 'And I could have been bitten by a snake!'

The pilot looks surprised. 'Oh, I hadn't thought of that.' He offers you a sympathetic smile. 'But yes, I'm sorry about the queen. Her life ended tragically and it must have been hard to see. But you did help her by going back. More than you can possibly imagine.'

'Where are we going for our last trip?'

'The Temple of Artemis at Ephesus. When Antipater of Sidon drew up his list of the Seven Wonders, he said this temple was the greatest wonder of them all.'

'Saving the best till last,' you say. 'Well, let's go then.'

CHAPTER 7:
THE TEMPLE OF ARTEMIS AT EPHESUS

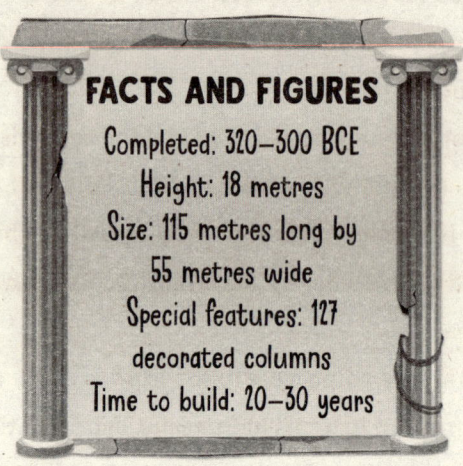

FACTS AND FIGURES

Completed: 320–300 BCE
Height: 18 metres
Size: 115 metres long by
55 metres wide
Special features: 127
decorated columns
Time to build: 20–30 years

WELCOME TO EPHESUS!

Ephesus was a large city located on the west coast of modern-day Turkey. Originally a Greek colony, it was famous for the magnificent Temple of Artemis, which was almost twice as big as any other Greek temple in the world. We're going to visit Ephesus during Roman times, when it was one of the most important cities in the empire. As well as the Temple of Artemis, Ephesus also had a famous library and an amphitheatre that could seat 25,000 people. They didn't just hold plays there, but gladiator fights too!

NO BOYS ALLOWED

Artemis was the Greek goddess of wild animals, hunting and the Moon. She was often associated with a legendary race of warrior women known as the Amazons. (You've probably heard of the superhero Wonder Woman – in the comic books, she's an Amazonian princess.) According to Greek legend, the Amazons wore men's clothing, rode on horses and fought with swords, spears, and bows and arrows. Basically they did all the things that male warriors were doing, except better. And their kingdom was strictly women-only – no men were allowed to enter.

Historians have often wondered how the Amazon legend started. Did these warrior women really exist? Unfortunately there's no evidence they did. In a land called Scythia near the Black Sea, however, archaeologists uncovered graves in which many women had weapons buried with them. While it doesn't seem they lived without men, it does suggest they were warriors and were perhaps the origin of these Greek stories.

HANDS OFF MY BELT!

The Amazons appear in lots of Greek myths. In one, they fight in a war between Greece and Troy, on behalf of Troy. This battle is described in a famous poem called The Iliad. In another story, they attack Athens when their queen, Hippolyta, is kidnapped by a Greek prince named Theseus, who wants to make a name for himself.

In a third story, they come up against Heracles, the mighty son of Zeus, who is sent on a mission to steal Queen Hippolyta's magic belt, a symbol of her power as queen. Heracles takes the belt after a fierce battle, which tragically ends in Hippolyta's death.

HERACLES: I tried to buy the belt online but they didn't have it.

HIPPOLYTA: Wrong Amazon.

THE TEMPLES OF ARTEMIS

The Wonder of the World we're going to visit is actually the third temple that was built on this site in Ephesus. We don't know anything about the first one, except that the Greeks believed it was built by the Amazons to worship their patron goddess, Artemis. At some point, it disappeared and was replaced by a second temple, constructed in 550 BCE by a super-rich and powerful king called Croesus.

That too, however, didn't survive. In 356 BCE, an ordinary Ephesian named Herostratus decided he wanted to do something that would make him famous. There were lots of ways he could do this: carve the most beautiful statue in the world; eat an entire cow at the Olympic Games; or invent a cool device like an invisible shield or a flying chariot. But all of these sounded like a lot of hard work, so Herostratus decided to burn down the Temple of Artemis instead.

The great temple was destroyed, and the Ephesians were forced to start building it all over again. It took them over twenty years until the third and final temple was completed in around 320 to 300 BCE.

I'm the most famous man in Ephesus.

Who's this guy?

Never seen him before in my life.

I bet that chariot doesn't even fly.

SURVIVE IN TIME

It's time for your final trip. I know by now you've probably had enough of perilous journeys to the Ancient Wonders and you'd rather stay home and watch TV, but I'm afraid that's not an option. This book entitles you to seven trips and seven trips are what you're getting.

Today our time machine is taking us to 120 CE, about 400 years after the third Temple of Artemis was constructed. Why 120 CE? Because the city of Ephesus reached new heights during this period of the Roman Empire. Using the power of their legions and the skills of generals such as Julius Caesar, the Romans had carved out one of the largest empires in history, covering much of Europe, North Africa, Turkey and parts of the Middle East. Ephesus in Turkey (or Asia Minor, as it was called then) was one of the most important cities in the eastern empire.

It's going to be an exciting visit to the Temple of Artemis. As the pilot mentioned, Antipater of Sidon thought it was the most wonderful wonder of all the wondrous Ancient Wonders.

But do try to be careful. The Romans had lots of nasty punishments for people they didn't like, including crucifixion. (That's the word for nailing people to crosses, in case you've never experienced it.) Having made it this far, it would be a shame for something to happen to you now.

Your mission is simple: to explore the Temple of Artemis. No special equipment needed this time – just your AI translator and your special watch – though it'll be hard to reach your watch if your hand is nailed to a cross.

***

For the seventh and final time, the time machine twists, turns and tumbles you to your destination. You've long since got used to its violent lurching, and on arrival, you step out as calmly as if you were setting off for a stroll in your local park. You're an experienced time-traveller by now.

You're in a busy street, and the machine has landed outside a stone building with a procession of people going in and out. It seems like a good place to start your adventure, so you step inside through a small door.

You find yourself in a room with rows of stone benches on three sides. People are sitting on the benches – some staring fixedly ahead, others turning to those next to them and chatting good-naturedly. You look for an empty spot and notice something unusual: there's a hole in the bench right where you're supposed to sit down. It almost looks like . . . and now you think of it, it definitely *smells* like . . . a toilet.

There are no barriers between the seats, which means you can see everyone doing their business, and, as far as you can tell, there is no toilet paper either. Instead of toilet paper, there's a kind of sponge on a stick designed for the same purpose. You have to dip the sponge in a stream of water in front of the benches to clean it off from the last person who used it.

You suppose it's interesting to see a Roman public toilet, but this is absolutely NOT one of the Seven Wonders of the Ancient World, or at least you hope not. You leave as quickly as you entered. But which way to go? Left will take you down the main street and right will take you towards the sea.

OPTION 1:
TURN DOWN THE MAIN STREET (PAGE 199)

OPTION 2:
TURN TOWARDS THE SEA (PAGE 197)

YOU DECIDE TO TURN TOWARDS THE SEA.

The first place you come to is the main marketplace, the agora, where the city's business is conducted. But today it's less busy than the street next to the agora, along which you find a great amphitheatre with a rising bank of stone seats. It's like the one you visited in Halicarnassus but much bigger. A long line of people are heading inside, chatting together in excited groups. It looks like some kind of event is about to start. A play, or something else?

Outside the amphitheatre, the streets are thronged with people. There are stalls selling all kinds of food: baked bread, meat skewers, olives, fruit and cheese. The most popular stall has golden buns glazed in honey and decorated with sliced nuts. They look delicious, and you can understand why there's a queue of people waiting to buy them.

There's no sign of the Temple of Artemis, so you decide to ask a local for directions.

THE TEMPLE OF ARTEMIS AT EPHESUS **197**

You notice a blond, blue-eyed boy, a little smaller than you, stuck behind the crowd at the stall.

'Hello, do you know where the Temple of Artemis is?'

The boy gives you a toothy grin. 'Sure, I can take you there! But I want a honey cake first. Can you pass me one? You're taller than me.'

That seems easy enough. As you're reaching over towards the stall, you hear a great roar from the amphitheatre. That sounds more dramatic than a play. What's going on?

OPTION 1:
CHECK OUT THE
AMPHITHEATRE
(PAGE 206)

OPTION 2:
PASS THE BOY A HONEY
CAKE (PAGE 202)

YOU DECIDE TO TURN DOWN THE MAIN STREET.

You don't get far before you're swept up in a group of people heading into a large marble building. They include cheerful families with children, so you're sure it's not a toilet this time. Nobody goes to a public toilet as a family outing. Could it be the Temple of Artemis?

Inside a spacious foyer, the men and boys go in one direction and the women and girls in another. Curious, you follow on behind and find yourself in a room where, without any warning, everybody starts taking their clothes off. Is it just your imagination or do ancient people spend a lot of time naked in public? This can't be the Temple of Artemis. In fact, it's a Roman bathhouse.

Well, you think to yourself, you did get pretty dusty in Alexandria, so maybe a bath is just what you need. You strip off and join the other patrons.

You start in a room called the *tepidarium*. It has warm air and heated floors but no bath. People sit around and relax, chatting in small groups. You stay for a while before moving to the next room, the *caldarium*, which has spacious, open baths filled with steaming water. You find a curved metal tool for scraping the dirt from your body and give yourself a clean before slipping slowly into the bath. This is going to be lovely!

Aaargh! Not lovely! Hot, hot, hot! You jump out and try again, one toe at a time, wondering how the other people can stand it. They must have skin like leather. For a few minutes you feel as though you're boiling alive in the water and, before long, decide you've had enough relaxation.

You take yourself into the third and final room. This one feels cooler, and you lower yourself into the pool with relief, guessing it's a more bearable temperature. Another mistake. Cold, cold, cold! It's the *frigidarium*: a cold bath for refreshing yourself.

Quickly jumping out of the icy water, you decide Roman baths are not for you and turn your mind back to the Temple of Artemis. While you were in the tepidarium, you overheard a conversation about a famous library not far from the bathhouse. Could it have a map that will show you where the temple is? Or do you want to explore the area around the sea and look for it there?

OPTION 1:
GO TO THE LIBRARY
(PAGE 208)

OPTION 2:
TURN TOWARDS THE SEA
(PAGE 197)

EVERYTHING YOU WANTED TO KNOW ABOUT ROMAN BATHS AND TOILETS

Sitting together on benches to go to the loo might sound, well, a bit awkward – but the Romans were serious about hygiene, and their technology was very advanced for the time. They built long series of stone arches called aqueducts, which carried water to their cities from faraway rivers, and they made underground sewers to keep the city streets clean. As well as the public lavatories that anyone could use, wealthy people also had toilets in their homes. Some had baths too, but for most citizens, bathing was done in public baths like the one you visited. The bathhouse was a social place for meeting friends and exchanging news and gossip.

YOU DECIDE TO PASS THE BOY A HONEY CAKE.

You reach out between the press of bodies and pluck one of the golden buns from the stall. The blue-eyed boy takes it with a grateful smile and offers you a bite. You accept, tasting herbs, raisins, nuts and honey. Delicious!

'Oi! You haven't paid!'

The shopkeeper is glaring at you fiercely between the other customers. How have you not learned your lesson yet about taking things from market stalls? You apologize and turn to your new friend, only to see him running off as fast as he can.

'I have no money! I'm sorry!' he shouts behind him.

You stand frozen in fear as a hand suddenly grabs your wrist. Two burly Roman soldiers have appeared from nowhere.

'Yes, that's the thieving little urchin!' the shopkeeper calls out.

The soldiers glance down at your sorry figure and drag you away from the stall. You start to explain about the boy, but they are already discussing your punishment.

'What shall we do then? The usual flogging for petty theft?' one says.

His colleague considers this. 'Well, there's a special celebration in town today. Public games at the amphitheatre, lots of food and drink . . . Maybe we can make an exception this time and –' you start to breathe a sigh of relief – 'crucify it instead.'

'Wait . . . what?' you yelp.

'Brilliant idea! Much quicker! I'll tell the magistrate!' the first soldier enthuses. 'Crucifying a child for stealing a honey cake! And I thought this day couldn't get any better!'

'Best job in the world!'

This is not looking good. Is there a way you can get out of it?

OPTION 1:
ACTIVATE YOUR SPECIAL
WATCH (PAGE 219)

OPTION 2:
OFFER TO PAY BY
WORKING AT THE STALL
(PAGE 211)

FIVE INTERESTING WAYS TO DIE IN ANCIENT ROME

The Romans had creative ways of punishing criminals. Here are some of their favourites:

1. Crucifixion
You wouldn't actually be crucified just for stealing a honey cake, but it was a common way of punishing serious criminals or rebellious slaves. Nailed to a wooden cross by your hands and feet, it could take a long time to die.

2. Fighting with wild animals
Prisoners could be sent into the arena to fight wild animals such as lions or bears while people watched. They were very one-sided fights.

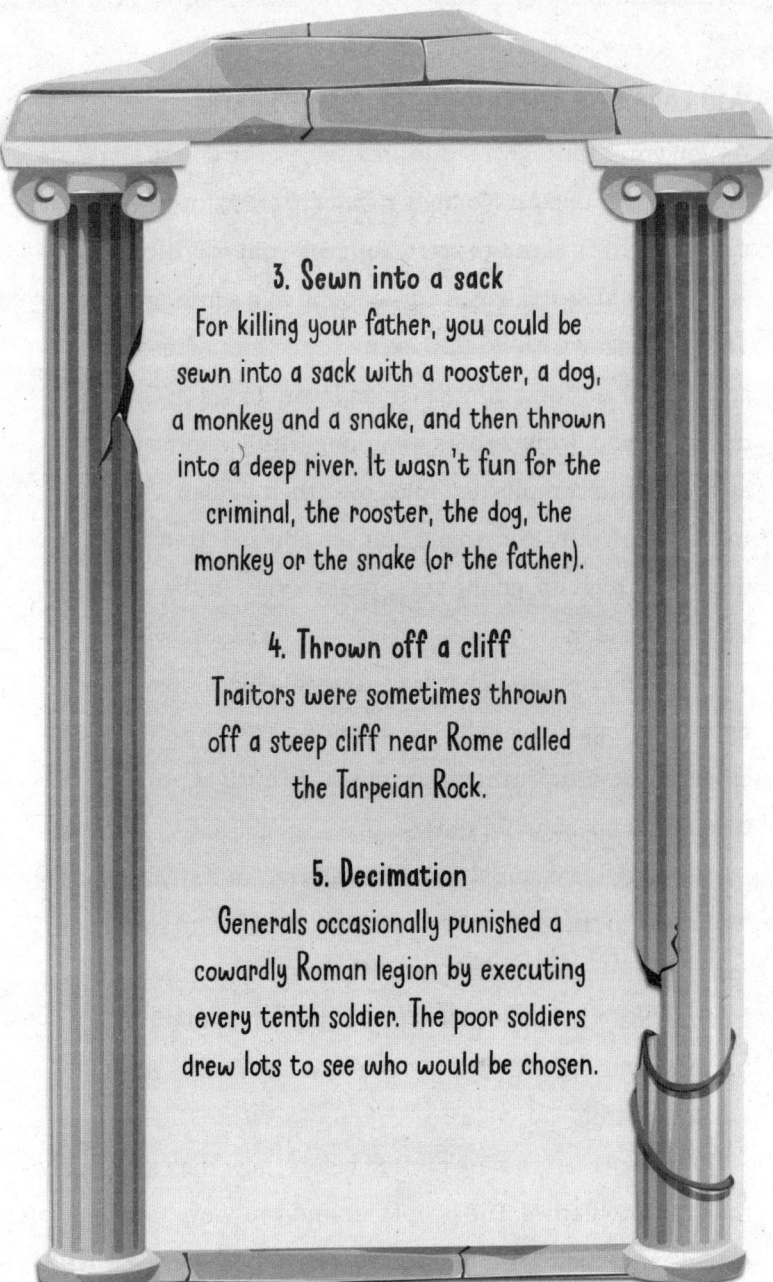

3. Sewn into a sack

For killing your father, you could be sewn into a sack with a rooster, a dog, a monkey and a snake, and then thrown into a deep river. It wasn't fun for the criminal, the rooster, the dog, the monkey or the snake (or the father).

4. Thrown off a cliff

Traitors were sometimes thrown off a steep cliff near Rome called the Tarpeian Rock.

5. Decimation

Generals occasionally punished a cowardly Roman legion by executing every tenth soldier. The poor soldiers drew lots to see who would be chosen.

YOU DECIDE TO CHECK OUT THE AMPHITHEATRE.

As you enter through a stone archway, you're greeted by a cacophony of cheers. No, they're not cheering for you, but for the show that's about to start. You pick your way along the steep bank of seats, which curve round in a semi-circle. They're packed with 25,000 excited spectators dressed in a variety of clothing: some men and women are in Greek dress like you, while others wear long white lengths of cloth arranged into complicated folds over their bodies. These are togas, which only Roman citizens are allowed to wear. You find a seat high up, giving you a perfect view of the sandy floor of the arena.

Three figures emerge from a tunnel below you: a round figure in a toga, flanked by two towering Roman soldiers. The crowd bursts into enthusiastic applause until the man in the toga raises his hand for quiet.

'Good citizens of Ephesus!' he calls out in a strong voice. 'Welcome to the games! We have an incredible show for you today! Thrilling re-enactments of battles! Fearsome lions from Africa! And, above all –' he pauses for dramatic effect, his face swelling with pride – 'the finest gladiators in the whole empire!'

If the spectators were excited before, now they look ready to burst into flames. The people around you jump to their feet, waving their arms deliriously. The official gives a wave before leaving the arena. From a tunnel on the other side, a pair of quite different figures now emerge: one man is wearing a helmet and holding a sword and shield, while the other has no helmet or shield but carries a net in one hand and a three-pronged trident in the other. The two muscly gladiators salute the crowd before getting into position opposite each other. They settle into fighting poses, weapons raised.

You feel your heart thumping inside your chest. Do you want to watch the men fight, or leave the arena before blood is spilled?

OPTION 1:
WATCH THE GLADIATORS FIGHT (PAGE 215)

OPTION 2:
LEAVE THE ARENA (PAGE 212)

YOU DECIDE TO GO TO THE LIBRARY.

It's an impressive structure with two levels supported by tall marble columns. Four female statues representing Wisdom, Intelligence, Knowledge and Virtue gaze out from the entrance. You join a handful of visitors passing through the doors and find yourself in an open hall with beautiful mosaics on the floor. Above you is a balcony running all the way around the walls. It's a magnificent space and, for a change, everybody is wearing clothes. Even ancient people don't get naked in a library.

But one thing puzzles you. Where are the books? You move to one of the walls and see it's lined with alcoves with small wooden cupboards inside. A bald man comes up and opens one of the cupboards, which you see is filled with paper scrolls. He takes a scroll before sitting down on a stone chair and opening it up. He starts to read the handwritten script, which your AI device informs you is ancient Greek. You wonder what it's about, but judging by the man's

Seriously?

serious and studious expression, you doubt it's got anything fun like wizards, superheroes or time-travelling kids in it.

You need to find a map of Ephesus, so you follow the bald man's example and randomly pull out a scroll from one of the cupboards. Unfortunately you're not very careful and the other scrolls, which were balancing on top of the one you pulled, all come tumbling out, landing on the stone floor with a clatter.

Immediately all eyes are on you and a furious librarian starts to stride towards you. What do you do? Make a quick getaway and head back in the other direction towards the sea, or be brave and ask the angry librarian for a map?

OPTION 1:
TURN RIGHT TOWARDS
THE SEA (PAGE 197)

OPTION 2:
ASK THE LIBRARIAN
ABOUT A MAP
(PAGE 211)

ANCIENT CHILDREN'S STORIES

Do you know the story of 'The Hare and the Tortoise'? How about 'The Boy Who Cried Wolf'? Or 'The Goose that Laid the Golden Eggs'? These stories were created by a Greek writer named Aesop, who was said to have been born around 620 BCE. One book about his life even says he put his stories in the Library of Croesus, an earlier version of the library you're standing in now! You couldn't borrow books from a Roman library because they were too valuable, but anyone could enter and read for free.

THAT WASN'T A GOOD OPTION. HOW VERY UNFORTUNATE.

Getting into trouble while time-travelling is never a good idea, and when it comes to the Roman Empire, it's a really bad idea. But don't worry – you know the drill by now! The following letter will be provided to anyone interested in your whereabouts:

Dear parent, guardian, teacher or interested person,

It is with great regret that we inform you of the loss of [insert name here] in Ephesus. It appears they failed to return to the transport vehicle by the scheduled time. Although at this point it is difficult to know where (or when) they are, we can assure you we are doing everything in our power to find them.

Please be aware that [insert name here] was clearly warned of the risks involved with their journey. The company cannot, therefore, take any financial responsibility for their disappearance.

Yours sincerely,

Intrepid Explorers Inc.

Think you could do better next time?
Go back and start again on page 194!

YOU DECIDE TO LEAVE THE ARENA.

You squeeze past the spectators in the packed seats. As you reach the exit, a wild cheer goes up, so loud it seems to make the ground shake. Distracted, you turn around and crash head first into a large figure. You hit the ground in a heap, as if you'd collided with a solid brick wall. A massive hand reaches down and picks you up by your tunic.

'You need to look where you're going. You could have injured me,' he says gruffly.

Injured him? He's about twelve feet tall and looks like a rhino standing on two legs.

'You can make up for it by helping me get ready,' he continues. 'Come with me.'

You have no choice but to obey, since he still has hold of your tunic. He takes you down a flight of winding steps, which emerge into a dim tunnel lit by torches on one side. It smells of sweat and dirt, and echoes with deep grunts and groans. For a moment you're confused about where you are, but then a raucous cheer rings out from above and you realize you're under the arena. This must be where the gladiators wait for their turn to fight. You're led into a dingy room where three men are warming up with stretches and sword swings.

'These are my good friends: Magnus the Bear-Slayer, Thrax the Bringer of Death and Verus the Beast of Sicily,' the rhino says. 'And I'm Maximus the Pain-Giver. Now, which one of us would you like to fight first?'

Your stomach lurches in terror. 'F . . . fight?'

Maximus lets out a booming laugh. 'Ha ha! I'm only joking. No, we just need you to polish our weapons with oil so they're in perfect condition for the games. Here, do mine first.'

Magnus the Ant-Slayer? Magnus the Cuddle-Giver? I don't know, they just don't sound right.

How about Magnus the Biscuit-Sharer?

He passes you his sword, and both the weapon and your arm hit the floor with a clang. When you try to lift it, it feels like trying to pick up a car. The four gladiators shake their heads.

'Perhaps you're not suited to helping gladiators,' Maximus muses. 'But there are some other jobs you could do instead. For instance, we need someone to feed to the lions.'

Feed to the lions? Surely he means feed the lions. That could be an exciting job, but do you have time?

OPTION 1:
TRY OUT YOUR NEW JOB
(PAGE 211)

OPTION 2:
ACTIVATE YOUR SPECIAL
WATCH (PAGE 219)

REAL-LIFE GLADIATORS

Being a gladiator was a very hard and dangerous profession. Although some men chose to become gladiators for glory and riches, most were slaves who didn't have a choice. If they were great fighters, however, they could become famous, like sports stars today. Two of the most celebrated were Flamma, who was only defeated four times in his thirteen-year career (being defeated didn't always mean you were killed — it cost a lot of money to train a gladiator and their lives weren't wasted easily), and Spartacus. Spartacus won fame in the arena, but then gained even more fame after he escaped and started an uprising against Rome. His army of slaves won several battles against well-trained Roman legions, but eventually they were defeated. Spartacus was killed in the battle and his supporters were crucified.

YOU DECIDE TO WATCH THE GLADIATORS FIGHT.

The fighter with the shield and sword is known as a *murmillo*. He looks like a walking tank and seems to have a huge advantage with his size, strength and shield. Facing him is a *retiarius*, a gladiator armed with a net and trident. He will have to rely on speed and cleverness. He has to avoid the heavy sword thrusts of his opponent and try to tangle him in his net. As the crowd fall silent in anticipation, the two men circle each other, waiting for the right moment to attack.

Suddenly there's a roar as the retiarius flings his net forward as quick as a flash. The murmillo is ready and slashes it away with his sword. The larger man charges forward, holding his shield in front of him and thrusting out his sword. The retiarius dodges at the last moment, poking with his trident. It hits the murmillo's shield with a clang and the spectators let out a gasp of excitement.

Now it's the sword that's swinging, cutting through the air towards the unarmoured retiarius's chest. The agile fighter spins away just in time to avoid a deadly blow, but the sword's tip catches his shoulder and draws blood. The crowd let out a deafening cheer, urging the murmillo on to finish the job. He swings hard again, but this time his opponent anticipates the move. He flicks his net forward and entangles the sword, then stabs his trident forward. It pierces the murmillo's thigh and the massive fighter goes down to one knee, bleeding from the deep wound. The retiarius knows he's won. He holds his trident to his opponent's neck and calls for him to surrender. Defeated, the murmillo drops his sword.

The crowd roar and stamp their feet, applauding the brave fighters for their display. You're relieved to see the defeated gladiator get up from the floor. He hangs his head and limps out of the arena, while the retiarius drinks in the glory.

Well, that was exciting, but also very scary. You don't think you can stomach watching another fight, and you get up to leave. Just then, you catch sight of a flash of blond hair disappearing down the steps. It's the young boy from the honey cake stall! He knew where the Temple of Artemis was – is it worth following him?

OPTION 1:
FOLLOW THE BOY
(PAGE 217)

OPTION 2:
LEAVE THE ARENA
(PAGE 212)

YOU DECIDE TO FOLLOW THE BOY.

He scurries down the steps to exit the arena and you follow a few metres behind. He heads off down the busy main street, passing the honey cake stall. You feel a twinge of guilt that you didn't pass him one earlier. At that moment, he turns round and smiles when he sees you.

'You wanted to see the Temple of Artemis, didn't you? I'm heading there now if you want to join me.'

You go with him gratefully, the two of you strolling along the street until you leave the crowds behind. It turns out that the temple is a mile outside the city. When you finally reach it, the first things you notice are the columns. You've already seen how much the ancient world loved columns, and the Temple of Artemis is no exception! There are 127 of them spaced out along all four sides, each more than eighteen metres high. Made of shining marble, they look like a forest of white trees.

The columns hold up a massive triangular roof. On the front façade there are carved pictures of female warriors wielding spears and shields. These are the famous Amazons who were believed to have founded the first temple many hundreds of years ago. With no one around to stop you, you climb up a set of fourteen steps to enter the building, finding yourself in a truly massive space. It's 115 metres long and 55 metres wide – bigger than a football pitch – and is surrounded by a double line of columns on each side.

There are exquisite carvings on the base of each column depicting scenes from Greek mythology. You see epic battles between gods and giants and heroes and monsters. At the far end of the temple is a statue of Artemis herself. She has the face of a goddess, but her legs are carved with images of wild animals like stags, bulls and lions. The perfect carvings for the goddess of wild beasts. She is painted with bold, bright colours of red, blue and gold.

You and the boy happily explore the temple together until suddenly your watch starts to flash. It's the pilot: time to get back to the time machine. You say goodbye to your companion and thank him for taking you to the final Wonder of the Ancient World.

'Where are you going now?' he asks.

You smile. 'More like *when*.'

OPTION 1:
RETURN TO THE TIME MACHINE. IT'S TIME TO GO HOME! (PAGE 220)

OPTION 2:
RETURN TO THE TIME MACHINE. IT'S TIME TO GO HOME! (PAGE 220)

YOU DECIDE TO ACTIVATE YOUR SPECIAL WATCH AND RETURN TO THE TIME MACHINE.

Unfortunately you didn't manage to complete your mission of exploring the Temple of Artemis. You approach the machine with your head bowed.

'Sorry you weren't able to see the final Wonder of the World,' the pilot says, as you strap yourself into your seat. 'But did you enjoy your seven trips with us? Were they everything you expected?'

'Yes, but I didn't think they'd be quite so dangerous. There were an awful lot of different ways to get into trouble.'

'Your ticket is not refundable and the company does not accept any claims for compensation,' the pilot says firmly.

'I wasn't asking for compensation,' you say, huffing. 'Anyway, I think I'm ready to go home now.'

'Good, then tighten your seat belt. This might get bumpy.'

Feeling brave enough to give it another try?
Go back to page 194!

CONGRATULATIONS! YOU COMPLETED YOUR MISSION!

You explored the Temple of Artemis and didn't experience any of the interesting (and scary!) ways the Romans punished people. The pilot gives you a respectful nod as he lets you into the time machine.

'Well done on surviving your seven trips. That's a pretty rare achievement.'

'How rare?' you ask.

'Oh . . . very rare. I'd say only one child in . . .' He hesitates and scratches his forehead.

'One child in five? One in ten? One in a hundred?' you prompt, horrified.

'One child in . . . the entire history of our company, actually.'

You're not sure how to react to that. 'You mean I'm the first ever to survive?'

He nods. 'As I said, well done. Anyway, shall we go? I imagine you're hungry.'

After 2,120 years without dinner, you have to agree.

'Yes, I'm definitely hungry.'

You fasten your seat belt and close your eyes as the time machine whirrs into life. What's the first thing you'll eat when you get home? You're thinking anything but locusts . . .

ARE YOU A BRAINY BOX?

Inside each adventure in this book, there were information boxes (like the one on page 20, for example). Were you paying attention to them? Take this Brainy Box quiz to find out!

(Warning: failure to score at least 12/14 will require you to go back in time and start again.)

I. **CHAPTER I: WHAT WAS THE FAVOURITE DRINK OF EGYPTIAN WORKERS WHO BUILT THE PYRAMIDS?**

   (a) water
   (b) beer
   (c) cola

2. **CHAPTER I: WHAT ORGAN DID THE EGYPTIANS PUT BACK INSIDE A MUMMY?**

   (a) the brain
   (b) the liver
   (c) the heart

3. **CHAPTER 2: IN BABYLON, WHAT PRINCIPLE WERE THE LAWS OF HAMMURABI BASED ON?**

   (a) an eye for an eye
   (b) a leg for an arm
   (c) a nose for a toe

4. **CHAPTER 2: WHICH BABYLONIAN TEMPLE IS RESPONSIBLE FOR YOU LEARNING A FOREIGN LANGUAGE AT SCHOOL?**

   (a) the Shrine of Marduk
   (b) the Pillar of Nebuchadnezzar
   (c) the Tower of Babel

5. **CHAPTER 3: WHAT WAS BANNED IN GREECE FOR A MONTH AROUND THE OLYMPIC GAMES?**

   (a) sports
   (b) school
   (c) war

6. **CHAPTER 3: WHAT DID THE OLYMPIC WRESTLING CHAMPION MILO EAT ALL BY HIMSELF?**

   (a) a cow
   (b) his opponent
   (c) the Statue of Zeus

7. **CHAPTER 4: WHAT WAS DAZZLING ABOUT THE BADASS QUEEN, ZENOBIA OF SYRIA?**

   (a) her sword
   (b) her armour
   (c) her teeth

8. **CHAPTER 4: IN 480 BCE, 10,000 GREEK SOLDIERS FOUGHT AGAINST HOW MANY PERSIANS?**

   (a) 25,000
   (b) 250,000
   (c) 2.5 million

9. **CHAPTER 5: WHAT IMPORTANT IDEA WAS BORN IN ATHENS IN 508 BCE?**

(a) democracy

(b) fast food

(c) science

10. **CHAPTER 5: HOW DID THE FAMOUS GREEK PHILOSOPHER SOCRATES DIE?**

(a) He was thrown off a cliff.

(b) He was forced to drink poison.

(c) He was run over by a horse.

11. **CHAPTER 6: WHAT WAS A UNIT OF 5,000 ROMAN SOLDIERS KNOWN AS?**

(a) a column

(b) a centurion

(c) a legion

12. **CHAPTER 6: WHAT NAME WAS GIVEN TO OCTAVIAN WHEN HE BECAME ROME'S FIRST EMPEROR?**

(a) Augustus

(b) Disgustus

(c) Vindictus

13. **CHAPTER 7: HOW WERE PEOPLE WHO MURDERED THEIR FATHERS PUNISHED IN ANCIENT ROME?**

(a) drowned in a sack

(b) crucified

(c) tickled

14. **CHAPTER 7: WHO WROTE THE STORY 'THE HARE AND THE TORTOISE'?**

(a) The Brothers Grimm

(b) Hans Christian Andersen

(c) Aesop

ANSWERS

1. b, 2. c, 3. a, 4. c, 5. c, 6. a, 7. c, 8. b, 9. a, 10. b, 11. c,
12. a, 13. a, 14. c

ARE YOU READY FOR YOUR NEXT ADVENTURE IN THE ROMAN EMPIRE?

COMING JUNE 2026

ABOUT THE AUTHOR

Dave Rear is a writer and lecturer who has spent his life reading, writing, and talking about history. While he hasn't time-travelled yet, it would be a convenient way to make him vanish. He lives in Tokyo with his wife and two kids, who — by law — are required to read all his books. They also wish he could time-travel.